Mommy CALLS

Dr. Tanya Answers Parents' Top 101 Questions About Babies and Toddlers

Tanya Remer Altmann, MD, FAAP

D0961889

American Academy of Pediatrics
DEDICATED TO THE HEALTH OF ALL CHILDREN™

AAP Publishing Staff

Director, Department of Marketing and Publications
Maureen DeRosa, MPA

Director, Division of Product Development
Mark Grimes

Manager, Consumer Publishing
Carolyn Kolbaba

Director, Division of Publishing and Production Services
Sandi King

Manager, Editorial Services
Kate Larson

Editorial Specialist
Jason Crase

Manager, Print Production Services
Leesa Levin-Doroba

Print Production Specialist
Shannan Martin

Manager, Art Direction and Production
Linda J. Diamond

Director, Division of Marketing
Jill Ferguson

Manager, Consumer Product Marketing and Sales
Kathleen Juhl

Director, Division of Sales
Robert Herling

Cover design by Cathi Stevenson, BookCoverExpress.com
Front and back cover photos by Joy Harmon, Wildflowers Photography
Book design by Linda J. Diamond
Mommy Calls was created by Tanya Remer Altmann, MD, FAAP, and Michelle L. Shuffett, MD.

Library of Congress Control Number: 2008920764
ISBN: 978-1-58110-295-6

The recommendations in this publication do not indicate an exclusive course of treatment or serve as a standard of medical care. Variations, taking into account individual circumstances, may be appropriate.

Statements and opinions expressed are those of the author and not necessarily those of the American Academy of Pediatrics.

Products are mentioned for informational purposes only. Inclusion in this publication does not constitute or imply a guarantee or an endorsement by the American Academy of Pediatrics.

Every effort is made to keep *Mommy Calls* consistent with the most recent advice and information possible.

CB0052
9-202/rep0414

5 6 7 8 9 10

What People Are Saying

Mommy Calls is a handy little book filled with nuggets of wisdom that are practical, clear, and to the point!

> Harvey Karp, MD, FAAP
> Creator of the DVD/book, *The Happiest Baby on the Block*

Dr. Tanya's book is a dream for parents—the next best thing to having your pediatrician living in your home for the first 3 years of your baby's life. She is not only talented and experienced, but her concise and utterly readable style will make this a staple on every parent's bookshelf.

> Samantha Ettus
> Author of *The Experts' Guide to the Baby Years* and mother of 2

Mommy Calls is like having a pediatrician available 24/7 to answer your questions. Dr. Tanya covers every topic a new parent could possibly need to know. Her friendly, informative style makes reading *Mommy Calls* a joy. Every parent should have this book close by at all times.

> Dr. Jenn Berman
> Marriage, family, and child therapist and author of *The A to Z Guide to Raising Happy, Confident Kids*

Mommy Calls is just what the doctor ordered! In her relaxed, reassuring manner and laced with gentle humor, Dr. Tanya Remer Altmann answers the typical questions that confound and even worry many parents of very young children….I look forward to keeping it on my shelf for use with clients and maybe with my own grandchildren someday.

>   Betsy Brown Braun
>   Child development specialist and author of *Just Tell Me What to Say: Sensible Tips and Scripts for Perplexed Parents*

Easy to read and organized by category, *Mommy Calls* answers the many questions that you have as a parent but may think are too trivial to call the pediatrician with. It's like having a pediatrician with you 24/7!

>   Bridget Swinney, MS, RD
>   Author of *Baby Bites* and *Eating Expectantly*

Experienced pediatricians are worth their weight in gold, and Dr. Tanya's book proves that point. The questions she answers are the most frequently asked and her answers are straightforward, knowledgeable, and easy to read at the same time. Parents will find comfort knowing her sage advice is close at hand.

>   Steven P. Shelov, MD, MS, FAAP
>   Editor in chief, *Caring for Your Baby and Young Child: Birth to Age 5*

Mommy Calls is extremely well written and informative.… I look forward to having this book in my arsenal to help prepare my new moms and fathers to be. This is a great, great book!

>   Jason A. Rothbart, MD
>   Obstetrician/gynecologist, Cedars-Sinai Medical Center

Table of Contents

Legend

In pediatrics, many situations change dramatically depending on the specific age of the child, so the answers to many common questions will vary by age. Therefore, in this book, the following symbols indicate when advice is specific to a certain age range:

Babies aged birth through 3 months

Newborn

Babies aged 4 months through 1 year

Infant

Children aged 1 through 3 years

Toddler

As with all advice, sometimes it's most important to call your pediatrician. The following symbol marks those moments:

Call your pediatrician

Acknowledgments

If it hadn't been for all of the help, support, and encouragement of my family, colleagues, and everyone at the American Academy of Pediatrics (AAP), *Mommy Calls* would not be in your hands.

It was only with the assistance of these people that I managed to finish writing *Mommy Calls* while seeing patients in my office, giving birth to my second son, and making several cross-country trips to appear on NBC's *Today* show—have breast pump, will travel.

Special thanks to the following colleagues, friends, and family members who played an important role in the upbringing of *Mommy Calls:*

Thank you to Michelle Shuffett, MD, for your years of dedication to this project. Without you, *Mommy Calls* wouldn't have been conceived. Also, thank you to my mentors at Mattel Children's Hospital at the University of California, Los Angeles, and my partners at Community Pediatric Medical Group—William Greene, MD, FAAP; David Scherr, MD, FAAP; Howard Goldstine, MD, FAAP; Robert Nudelman, MD, FAAP; Heather Cornett-Young, MD, FAAP; and Leslie Spiegel, MD, FAAP—who taught me how to care for children in the real world and helped *Mommy Calls* grow and develop. In addition, thank you to Marilyn Greene, who taught me how to parent effectively in my practice and at home, and Elisa Hirsch, whose breastfeeding advice has helped me guide patients and nurse my own 2 sons. A very special recognition belongs to Jennifer Shu, MD, FAAP, and Laura Jana, MD, FAAP, who went above and beyond in offering exceptional advice and contributions based on their personal experience as moms, pediatricians, and parenting book authors.

Thank you to the following physicians for their technical review and additions to my manuscript: Gwen O'Keefe, MD, FAAP; Angelee Reiner, MD, FAAP; Frank Greer, MD, FAAP; Patricia Treadwell, MD, FAAP; Robert Steele, MD, FAAP; Brynie Slome Collins, MD, FAAP; Andrew Shpall, MD; and Neela K. Sethi, MD, FAAP. Also, thanks to my son's pediatric dentist, Yael Bar-Zion, DDS.

I want to express my appreciation to the AAP Department of Marketing and Publications, including Mark Grimes, Carolyn Kolbaba, and Kathleen Juhl, who helped deliver *Mommy Calls* into the world.

Last, but definitely not least, thank you to my family— Clifford Numark, who taught me how to write, and Melissa Curry Remer, for her book review and numerous hours spent caring for my boys. A heartfelt thanks to my sister, Candace Remer Katz, MD, an allergist and mom who keeps me up-to-date on asthma and allergy topics and added immensely to this book while caring for her own newborn and toddler.

I owe my life and many accomplishments to my parents and grandparents who always support me and encourage me to reach for my dreams. Mom and Dad, thank you for reading *Mommy Calls* in its entirety and offering invaluable advice as experienced and successful parents and grandparents.

A huge debt of gratitude to my in-laws, who often babysat so I could work and who are more loving and accommodating than I could have ever dreamed.

Finally, thank you to my husband and the best daddy ever, who really does everything and without whom I could never do all that I do. We have 2 wonderful sons, Avrick and Collen, who have taught me more about pediatrics and parenting than I could ever learn at the office and who are constantly making me smile with a new adventure every day. I am proud to be their mommy.

Introduction

Mommy Calls was born one busy night at Mattel Children's Hospital at the University of California, Los Angeles (UCLA), while I was caring for sick children with my good friend and fellow resident, Michelle Shuffett, MD. As pediatricians in training, part of the job was to provide telephone advice on a whole host of health and parenting concerns. While these calls came from moms, dads, grandparents, and other caregivers, we called them "mommy calls." That night, after answering what seemed to be dozens of calls on the same topic, I began tracking the questions parents ask. Over the years, I've added to that list as my clinical experiences have grown and as I've become a mother myself. Along with input from parents and pediatricians across the country, I've compiled what I consider to be the 101 most common questions parents ask their pediatrician in a simple, concise, and easy-to-read format.

Mommy Calls focuses on your child from birth through age 3 years and includes subjects such as feeding, illnesses, and sleeping. *Mommy Calls* is meant to answer not only the questions you have today, but those you are likely to have at 3:00 am tomorrow! *Mommy Calls* provides practical information, advice, important tips, a little humor, and best of all, it fits in your baby bag. So before you pick up the phone to call your pediatrician, check out *Mommy Calls* for your answer.

In pediatrics, many situations change dramatically depending on the specific age of the child, so it's no surprise that the answers to many common questions will vary by age.

Therefore, in this book, babies aged birth through 3 months are called *newborns* and are indicated by a pacifier (); babies aged 4 months through 1 year are called *infants* and are indicated by a rattle (); and children aged 1 through 3 years are called *toddlers* and are indicated by blocks (). Symbols are used to make it easy to find the right advice for your child—they are explained by the Legend on page ix. As with all advice, sometimes it's most important to call your pediatrician. I've indicated those moments with a telephone symbol ().

Also, the information and advice in this book apply equally to children of both sexes, except where noted. To indicate this, the use of masculine and feminine pronouns is alternated throughout.

I hope you find *Mommy Calls* helpful, but don't forget that you know your child best. You will undoubtedly come up with questions not addressed in this book. That's the nature of having kids! If ever you find yourself with unanswered questions, no matter how small or silly they may seem, go ahead and ask. And whenever you have more serious concerns, remember that no book, *Mommy Calls* included, can ever take the place of direct medical advice—you should never hesitate to call your pediatrician. After all, that's what we're here for—even at 3:00 am!

CHAPTER 1

Basic Baby Care

"The baby is here...now what do I do?"

If you're reading this book, congratulations on the arrival of your baby! Chances are you're either getting a good head start in anticipating what lies ahead, or you've already made it through your hospital stay and are now home with your new little bundle of joy. Admittedly, some days may be more joyful, or at least more peaceful, than others. Whether you're trying to figure out why your baby is crying (is she hungry, wet, tired...ugh!) or you're attempting to get her dressed and out the door for her first doctor's appointment (don't forget that new baby bag), you will quickly realize that your life has now changed...forever.

Even though you've eagerly awaited and geared up for this wonderful change for the last 9 months (if not more), you are likely to still find yourself needing some guidance now that your baby has actually arrived and you've become a parent. In the hospital you probably had lots of help—nurses, lactation consultants, doctors—all at your beck and call. You may already have read all the must-have parenting books and spent many evenings on the phone with your mother and girlfriends. You thought you were prepared. But nothing can ever completely prepare you for the crazy but exciting ride ahead. During the first few days at home with a newborn, most parents have questions—usually lots of them! Here are some of the answers.

(If it is sleep, feeding, poop, fever, or skin-related answers you're looking for, rest assured that these very important newborn topics are covered in their own chapters.)

Out and About

1. When do I need to bring my baby in for a checkup?

In general, it's a good idea to see your pediatrician within 2 days of leaving the hospital. In decades past, longer hospital stays allowed babies to be observed for about a week after delivery. This also gave parents more time to gain some hands-on newborn experience. Nowadays, the first checkup is typically scheduled soon after discharge (within your baby's first week) to make sure your baby is feeding, peeing, and pooping well; isn't jaundiced (see question #71, page 108); and hasn't lost too much weight. All babies initially lose weight after they are born and most regain their birth weight by 2 weeks of age. This early visit is especially useful because a majority of babies spend only 2 to 3 days, at most, in the hospital after birth. That's certainly a lot to learn in a short time. How your baby is feeding, pooping, and behaving will dictate how often he needs to be seen in the first few weeks.

Remember that after being sleep-deprived for 72 hours you may barely remember your name, let alone the questions you thought of in the middle of the night, so write them down as you think of them. Allow plenty of time to pack up (see Dr. Tanya's Tip: Baby Bag Essentials below), get out

---

DR. TANYA'S TIP
Baby Bag Essentials

Babies need lots of stuff—all the time. So prepare an extra baby bag…or two. Give one to anyone else who will be caring for your baby. That way all the necessities will be available if an outing takes longer than expected. A well-stocked baby bag should include the following:

- Five diapers (at least)
- Changing pad
- Baby wipes
- Diaper cream
- Plastic bags for dirty diapers or clothes
- Formula, bottle, and nipple (if formula feeding)
- Burp cloths
- Bottle of water (to mix formula, clean up messes, or drink yourself)
- Change of clothing (for baby and you)
- Blanket
- Pacifier (if your baby uses one)
- Infants' acetaminophen (Tylenol)
- Hand sanitizer
- List of important information—pediatrician's phone number, recent weight of baby, allergies (if any), immunization records

Don't forget to restock items as they are used so you're always ready to go anywhere, anytime.

the door, and arrive at your appointment—it can take some time to get used to moving about with a newborn!

After your hospital follow-up visit, regular well-baby examinations for the first year are usually scheduled at 2 weeks, 1 month, 2 months, 4 months, 6 months, 9 months, and 12 months. Of course, this schedule varies slightly from doctor to doctor. It may seem like you are always on your way to the pediatrician, but every well-baby examination is important. Your doctor will examine your baby from head to toe, check his growth, evaluate his development, look for signs of illness, and provide advice for keeping your little one healthy, happy, and safe. In addition, there may be specific tests and immunizations recommended depending on the age of your baby at each visit.

 You can always schedule an appointment for your baby if any specific problems or concerns arise between well-child examinations.

2. When can we take our newborn out?

Whether you're thinking of going outside, inside, or high up in the sky, a good rule of thumb is to stay away from crowds of people until your baby is 6 to 8 weeks of age if at all possible. This is because a newborn's immune system is still maturing, which leaves her more susceptible to catching colds as well as becoming seriously ill very quickly. Avoid any closed areas where your baby could be exposed to lots of people who may be sick such as the grocery store, mall, movie theaters, parties, or airplanes. During the winter especially, it's best to assume that everyone is contagious—some people may not show outward symptoms but can still spread germs! Whenever possible, don't let anyone who is obviously ill near your baby, keep young children away because they tend to be even less able to keep their hands and germs to themselves, and try to decrease the number of people who touch, breathe on, and cough on your baby.

Now that you know what to avoid, going outside is fine. Dress your baby appropriately (see Fun Fact: Is Baby Too Hot or Too Cold? below) and enjoy a stroll outside.

FUN FACT
Is Baby Too Hot or Too Cold?

You can't really know—unless you carry around a thermometer everywhere you go (which isn't realistic or recommended)! That's because babies don't always sweat or shiver when you might expect them to, and they can't yet tell you how they feel. The general rule is that babies should wear as many layers as you are wearing. It's all right to add one more layer if it makes you (or seems to make your baby) more comfortable. It's not necessary to change the thermostat in your house just because you have a newborn; just dress him appropriately. If it is a hot day and you are only wearing a T-shirt and shorts, your baby should be OK in a onesie. If it is cooler out and you need a sweater and jacket, dress your baby the same. A hat is always a good idea—if it stays on! When it's cold, babies lose body heat from their heads, and when it's hot, a hat will protect them from the sun.

3. What about taking my baby on an airplane?

Keep your flyboy or flygirl on the ground until 6 to 8 weeks of age if at all possible. The danger is not the airplane itself, but the possible contact with ill individuals (see question #2, pages 4–5). Otherwise, the airplane poses no risk other than potential ear discomfort. The ear canals in babies are narrower and more curved than adults, so pressure changes during takeoff and landing (landing more so than takeoff) can sometimes cause pain. Breastfeeding, bottle-feeding, or sucking on a pacifier is often soothing during these periods because sucking and swallowing can help equalize the pressure and decrease the pain. Wait until you are sure the plane is about to take off or start its descent so your baby doesn't fill up and stop sucking too soon. Another tip that may ease discomfort is to give the appropriate dose of acetaminophen (Tylenol) about 30 minutes prior to take-off and, if the flight is longer than 4 hours, again prior to landing (see Acetaminophen [Tylenol] Dosing Chart and Ibuprofen [Motrin or Advil] Dosing Chart on page 81).

DR. TANYA'S TIP
Keeping Baby Healthy

Allow older siblings to gently touch or kiss your baby's toes instead of her face or hands. This will help protect your newborn from catching any illnesses that your older ones may bring home. You can also appoint your older children to be hand-washing monitors to make sure that all visitors wash their hands before holding the baby—and that's a doctor's order!

Crying

4. Aaahh! My baby won't stop crying—I can't take it anymore! Is this much crying (and my frustration) normal?

Babies cry! When they're not sleeping, eating, or pooping, they're crying! They cry when they are hungry, wet, cold, hurt, or for no apparent reason at all. If it seems like hours every day, you may be right. On average, newborns cry up to 2 hours a day, and over the first few months they may cry even more. As you get to know your baby better, you may learn to distinguish her cries and what they mean. Once a baby has been fed, burped, changed, and checked to make sure nothing is hurting her, it's generally OK to let her cry for a little while. It may just be her way of blowing off steam, so give her the chance to just let it all out.

One practical approach to calming crying babies was developed by Harvey Karp, MD, FAAP. In his *The Happiest Baby on the Block* DVD, he demonstrates the 5 Ss: swaddling, side/stomach positioning while awake, shushing, swinging, and sucking. Another S I like to add is singing a song (your baby won't care if you can't carry a tune). Some babies also enjoy moving around, so hold your baby and dance or go for a walk. It may help both of you.

 Call your pediatrician if your baby has high-pitched or excessive crying or is truly inconsolable (the crying won't stop no matter what you do), since severe crying can be a sign of illness.

5. Is a pacifier OK?

Ah, the great "paci" debate. Here are the pros and cons.

Pros

- **Decreased risk of sudden infant death syndrome (SIDS)**

  Why? We don't know for sure, but some experts believe that the sucking stimulates the breathing center in the brain, while others think that the paci itself helps keep the airway open. In either case, the evidence is strong enough that the American Academy of Pediatrics now suggests that it is protective for a pacifier to be used when placing an infant to sleep during the first year of life, but should not be reinserted once the infant is asleep. If nursing, you can wait until breastfeeding is well established before introducing a pacifier.

- **Babies soothe themselves by sucking**

  Your breast is not meant to be a pacifier! If you have a baby with a strong urge to suck or a fussy baby who has been fed, burped, and changed, why not try the paci and see if it calms him down?

Cons

- **Early use may interfere with breastfeeding**

  It is sometimes difficult to identify and understand your baby's cues with a paci in his mouth, not to mention easier to overlook his hunger cues. Additionally, some infants may get confused since sucking on a pacifier (or even bottle) involves a slightly different action than for breastfeeding.

- **Overuse**

  Infants quickly get used to the paci to soothe themselves and aid in sleep—a habit that is often hard to break down the road. Older infants who use pacifiers are more prone to picking up colds because they are accustomed to constantly sucking and mouthing objects (the usual entry point for germs). In addition, paci use for longer than a year or two can interfere with tooth alignment and bite (just ask your dentist).

• **Increased risk of ear infections**
  There appears to be an association between pacifier use and increased ear infections. Some experts feel that the constant sucking on the pacifier can push extra fluid into the middle ear, increasing a baby's chance of developing an ear infection.

So, what do you do? If you have a fussy baby or a baby who has a strong urge to suck or you want to use a pacifier for falling asleep, wait until breastfeeding is well established and your baby is gaining weight, usually around 2 to 4 weeks. Between 4 and 6 months, your baby needs to develop his own self-soothing skills for daytime and nighttime. (He should be sleeping through the night now; if not, see Chapter 12, "Sleep," ASAP). Therefore, the best time to get rid of the paci is by 6 to 12 months of age. It's much easier to wean off the paci at this age rather than waiting until your older infant or toddler has declared it his security object and won't go to sleep without it. If you have an infant who doesn't like the paci, no need to force it.

Body Parts

Babies come with lots of parts. From head to toe there is a lot to cover, but no instruction manual to go along. Because this book is only meant to take on the most common questions, the list of parts covered may seem a bit random. Have other questions? Simply keep your own list and ask your pediatrician at your next well-baby visit. Should you find yourself with a more pressing question, pick up the phone.

6. I know my baby's belly button will be cute someday, but right now, it's just an alien-looking stump with a little yucky fluid around it. When will the cord fall off?

Don't worry—that umbilical cord stump won't be around forever. The stump will typically fall off around 1 to 3 weeks after birth. In the meantime, make sure to keep the area clean and dry. While cleaning with alcohol wipes used to be advised, most doctors now recommend to leave it alone— one less thing for you to do. That said, if the area gets dirty from poop or pee, go ahead and clean it with a baby wipe or a little rubbing alcohol on a cotton swab. Many caregivers also prefer to fold the diaper down in front (or buy newborn diapers specially designed with the belly button area cut out) so the cord doesn't get irritated or rubbed the wrong way.

It *is* normal to see some blood-tinged fluid or even dried blood a few days before and after the stump falls off. You may also notice a small, gooey lump (umbilical granuloma) at the base of the belly button. If this is the case, check with your pediatrician. The application of silver nitrate in the office can help a gooey cord dry up and heal. Alternatively, you can wipe it with rubbing alcohol several times a day for a few days. The granuloma should eventually go away and look like a normal belly button very soon. Sponge bathe your baby as needed until a day or two after the cord has fallen off and the belly button is dry and healed. Then you can start tub baths, rubber ducky and all—fun!

 Call your doctor if there is any redness on the skin surrounding the umbilical stump or if fluid or blood keeps leaking several days after the cord falls off.

FUN FACT
Nails...to Cut or Not to Cut?

I don't know what's worse—looking at the self-inflicted scratches babies often get from their nails or trying to cut those nails! An easier (and sometimes safer) option is to file your baby's nails. If you choose to clip and accidentally cut the skin (and we've all done it), apply pressure to stop any bleeding (which is usually minimal) and clean the wound well. Don't worry, your baby won't remember and you can continue manicuring as needed. Although rarely an issue, call your pediatrician if the area won't stop bleeding or shows signs of infection such as redness, swelling, or oozing. If possible, don't put gloves on his hands. He needs to touch things to learn about his environment.

7. My baby is congested. How can I help her breathe more comfortably?

Newborns and infants breathe mainly through their noses. Because their nasal passages are so tiny, a small amount of mucus can make a very loud noise. Even though they sound really congested, don't let the noise bother you unless it interferes with eating or sleeping. If the nasal congestion does interfere with your baby's ability to eat or sleep, touch base with your pediatrician. Feeding in an upright position or slightly elevating the head of the crib or bassinet may help. In addition, try the following techniques to relieve the congestion:

- Run a cool-mist humidifier or vaporizer in the room during sleep to keep the skin inside of the nose moist.
- Remove visible mucus by placing a drop of nasal saline in each nostril. Your baby may cough as the saline drips from the nose down the back of her throat—that's quite all right. Then gently suction out the mucus with a bulb syringe. If you can manage it or have an extra set of hands to help, hold one nostril closed while you suction the other. Try suctioning when your baby is in a slightly upright position as gravity can help the mucus drain. It's best not to suction more than a few times a day because it can irritate the inside of your baby's nose and worsen the congestion.
- Alternatively, after placing the saline in the nose, give your baby some tummy time. As she moves her head up and down (and even if she cries) the mucus will be more likely to drain out on its own.

Nasal saline drops can be bought or made (¼ tsp salt in 8 oz water), or you can even use a few drops of breast milk.

While most of the time nasal congestion is responsible for making a baby's breathing noisy, it is important to recognize signs of true troubled breathing that should be evaluated. A newborn normally breathes 30 to 60 times a minute (one breath every 1 to 2 seconds)—much faster than an older child or adult. If you feel like your baby is taking more than one breath per second, take a close look. Can you see her tummy or the space between the ribs moving in and out with each breath? Do you hear wheezing (a high-pitched whistle) or other extra noises with each breath? Is your baby's head bobbing as she breathes? Is she coughing? Is her nose flaring with each breath? Does her skin look blue?

 If the answer to any of these questions is "yes" or you simply can't tell the difference, call your pediatrician right away.

PEDIATRIC POINT
Preventing Flat Heads (aka Plagiocephaly)

Not only is it recommended that all healthy newborns be placed on their backs while sleeping, it's also a good idea to alternate the side to which your baby's head is turned when she is sleeping. This helps keep any one part of your baby's relatively soft skull bones from flattening under pressure. When awake, remember to give her plenty of supervised tummy time—an activity that will serve to strengthen her head, neck, and upper body as well.

8. Should I circumcise my baby? How do I take care of his penis after the procedure?

Overall, circumcision is an entirely personal decision, often determined by religious or ethnic beliefs. Deciding whether to circumcise is completely your call. While there are some known medical benefits to the procedure, including a decreased risk of developing urinary tract infections, sexually transmitted infections, or penile cancer, as well as a reduced risk that a sexual partner will acquire cervical cancer later in your son's life, it's worth keeping in mind that these conditions can often be prevented in other ways. Ultimately, the decision might be made because of something one of my mentors always said: "Johnny should look like his daddy!"

Circumcision has been around for thousands of years and although technique and aftercare instructions may vary, most circumcisions ultimately turn out looking essentially the same. How you care for the penis after the procedure depends on how the circumcision is performed and the preference of the specialist performing it.

Circumcisions generally fall into one of two types, both of which should be performed using some type of anesthesia so the newborn will not feel pain. The first uses the Plasti-bell, which is a ring that will fall off about a week after the circumcision. The second, and nowadays more commonly used, is a non–ring-type metal clamp called Gomco or Mogen. After the procedure, a thin piece of gauze is left covering the incision site. The gauze may stay in place for approximately 24 to 48 hours before falling off on its own. Sometimes your physician will have you replace the gauze. There will be some yellowish crusting or scabbing for about 7 to 10 days—don't worry, the skin will eventually heal and look normal. Until it is healed, your physician may recommend that you continue to cover the end of your baby's penis with petroleum jelly or another ointment at each diaper change to prevent the area from sticking to the diaper.

Call your pediatrician (or whoever performed your baby's circumcision) if your baby doesn't have a straight urine stream, if your baby hasn't peed for 8 hours after the circumcision (he may finally pee while you are dialing the phone), or if there is a lot of bleeding, pus, redness, or bruising.

9. How do I clean the foreskin if I don't circumcise my son?

Don't touch it! At least not yet anyway. Retracting and cleaning a baby's foreskin can actually cause small tears in the tissue, which can lead to adhesions and possible problems later in life. Instead, simply wash the outside of your baby's foreskin with water (with or without a mild soap) as you would any other part of his body. As boys get older (usually around age 2) they begin having nighttime erections; as a result, the foreskin will gently stretch on its own. Any adhesions that may have formed will separate. That said, plenty of normal little boys are unable to retract the foreskin until the age of 4 or 5, at which time you can teach your son how to gently clean the foreskin and the head of the penis underneath it. In due time, the foreskin will become easily retractable and your son will be old enough to care for it on his own.

 If there is ever any redness, swelling, or pain around your son's penis, bring it to the immediate attention of your pediatrician.

10. I found a red streak in my newborn's diaper. Could it be blood?

While it's certainly possible for a red streak in the diaper to be blood, it's usually not the most likely cause of such red discoloration.

- If the spot looks powdery, almost like blush makeup, it may be urate crystals (little particles in urine that are seen when babies drink less the first few days, often because mom's milk supply isn't fully in). Their appearance in the diaper is fairly common in the first few days of life and nothing to worry about.
- If you have a baby boy who was circumcised, there may be a dark yellow or bloody stain on the diaper from the site of circumcision. Examine the tip of the penis for signs of infection and bleeding—call your pediatrician if you see something suspicious (see question #8, pages 13–15).
- If you have a baby girl, it is possible that the red stain is actually blood, but not the kind that warrants concern. Baby girls can have withdrawal bleeding, similar to a woman's period. This occurs after birth because they are no longer exposed to mom's high estrogen levels. Again, it is nothing to worry about and will go away on its own.

 If you notice a red streak in your baby's diaper after the first week or have concerns at any time, you should see your baby's pediatrician. Try to bring a diaper with the stain if at all possible so your pediatrician can take a look.

CHAPTER 2

Breastfeeding
"Got breast milk?"

Many moms decide during pregnancy that they will nurse. Others are unsure, looking for more information. And some new mothers don't make their decision to breastfeed until they first hold their new little one against their chest, skin to skin, and that perfect baby with an adorable tiny mouth grasps their nipple and begins to suckle. Whenever you decide, feel good in knowing that you are making an amazing difference in your baby's life as well as your own.

Breastfeeding Basics

11. I want to breastfeed, but I'm worried I won't be able to do it. Where can I get help?

Although breastfeeding is natural, most babies aren't born experts (and neither are moms!). It may take days (or even weeks) for you and your little one to catch on, especially if your milk supply is a little slow to come in. Try not to get discouraged. Breastfeeding can take patience and hard work initially, but keep at it because it's worth it for your baby's health as well as your own. Don't be afraid to ask for help from day one, if not before. The American Academy of

PEDIATRIC POINT
Breast Milk Is Truly Best

While breastfeeding can admittedly seem demanding because of the significant time commitment required (believe me, I know!), the benefits are well documented and the experience is priceless. Mother's milk provides immunity against bacteria and viruses (less sick time for your little one), is easiest for your baby to digest, is uncommon for your baby to be allergic to, is less expensive (more money for cute baby clothes or a college fund), and requires no preparation time (just pull up shirt and feed). Studies show that breastfed babies have fewer ear, respiratory tract, and diarrheal infections. They are also at lower risk for many childhood diseases such as asthma, diabetes, and obesity. And breastfeeding is not just good for baby; it has many documented benefits for mom including a decreased future risk of cancer and diabetes as well as a faster return to pre-pregnancy weight. Breastfeeding burns 300 to 500 calories per day—the equivalent of a 3-mile run! After all you've gone through, you deserve this nice payback.

Pediatrics parenting book *New Mother's Guide to Breastfeeding* is an easy, enjoyable read to help guide new moms through nursing. You can talk to your pediatrician about the ins and outs of breastfeeding even before you deliver and ask for a list of recommended resources in your community. Many hospitals have lactation consultants available, and many postpartum and nursery nurses are also trained to help. Depending on where you live, there may be local lactation consultants available. Seek out an International Board Certified Lactation Consultant or contact your local

La Leche League chapter. Even one meeting with a lactation specialist in the first few days after having your baby can really pay off in the long run. Additionally, many mother support groups, breastfeeding centers, and stores have specialists available to provide resources and help with nursing.

```
PEDIATRIC POINT
Breastfeeding—the Official Word

The American Academy of Pediatrics (AAP) strongly sup-
ports breastfeeding as the optimal source of nutrition
through the first year of your baby's life. The AAP recom-
mends exclusively breastfeeding for 4 to 6 months, and
then gradually adding solid foods while continuing to
breastfeed at least until your baby's first birthday. Breast-
feeding can be continued for as long as you and your baby
desire.
```

12. When does my "real" milk come in?

The first 2 to 3 days after your baby is born you will produce yellowish, translucent fluid called colostrum. It contains easy-to-digest proteins, fats, vitamins, minerals, and antibodies to protect your baby from disease. It also contains a mild laxative to help your baby stool and get rid of bilirubin, the stuff that causes jaundice (see question #71, page 108). Frequent feedings the first few days, as well as rest (it's hard to find time, but you must), hydration, and proper nutrition, will help increase your milk production. After about 3 days of breastfeeding, you will begin to produce transitional milk. Your breasts may begin to feel fuller and tender. Continue to feed regularly and around 3 to 7 days you should see a little white milk dripping from the corners of your baby's mouth or your nipple. Congratulations, it's in!

 Call your pediatrician if your baby isn't having at least 3 to 5 wet diapers and 3 to 4 dirty diapers (sometimes one diaper may have both urine and stool combined) per day by 3 to 5 days of age. This may be a sign that your baby isn't getting enough colostrum or breast milk.

13. Is feeding on a schedule or on demand better for newborns?

Initially, babies should feed approximately 8 to 12 times in 24 hours, which is roughly every 2 to 3 hours. Breastfeed on demand as soon as your baby shows hunger cues such as rooting (turning her head and opening her mouth in search of your breast), smacking her lips, making suckling motions, or sometimes even crying (try not to wait for crying because it is a late sign of hunger). In the beginning she may nurse on each side for 20 to 30 minutes, but after your milk comes in and she is gaining weight, she will get more efficient and anywhere from 5 to 15 minutes per side may suffice. In general, the more often you breastfeed, the more milk you will produce because your body will make what it thinks your baby needs. While some babies will wake up every few hours on their own to feed, others may need a little coaxing. In the first few weeks, it's best to go with the flow and feed your baby as often as she wants, as this is the best way to establish a proper milk supply and ensure that your baby gets enough nutrition. Once your baby has regained her birth weight and is growing and developing well (usually by the 2-week checkup), you can let her sleep as long as she wants at night (turn off your alarm!). If at this point you want to try more scheduled feeds (such as every 3 hours), go ahead and see how your newborn responds. Just know that some babies like to "cluster feed" frequently during the day, eating as often as every hour or more, but stretch out their night-time feeds (more sleep for you!).

 If you are concerned about your newborn's feeding schedule or aren't sure if she is getting enough breast milk, see your pediatrician for a weight check between your normal well-baby examinations or whenever you feel it is needed.

PEDIATRIC POINT
Infant Vitamins

The American Academy of Pediatrics recommends that all breastfed infants be given vitamin D (400 IU) once daily (available in infant vitamin drops) starting within the first few days of life. This is because breast milk does not contain enough vitamin D and a mom's vitamin D does not pass into breast milk. Formula-fed babies drinking less than 32 oz a day of formula should receive vitamin D supplementation as well.

Pumping Pointers

14. Should I pump breast milk and give it in a bottle? When do I start?

If you plan to return to work, or ever want to go out to dinner and a movie without your baby in tow, then YES! Pumping and storing breast milk to be served in a bottle at a later time can also give others the opportunity to feed and bond with your baby (and can give you a much-needed break).

Once you have established a good breastfeeding routine and feel comfortable enough to add something else to your to-do list (often when your baby is around 2 or 3 weeks of age), you can begin to pump, store your breast milk, and introduce the bottle. If you wait too long you run the risk that your baby may not take a bottle and you'll get a panicked phone call from your sitter or child care provider to come right away! It's a good idea to have someone give your baby a bottle at least once every few days (even while you are at home) so he remains familiar with it.

Breast pumps are manual or electric, but if you plan to pump frequently, you may want to invest in an electric pump. If you aren't sure how long you are going to need it or want to try one out first, you can always rent one, instead of buying your own. Sound strange? Not really, once you discover that what you're really renting is the breast pump motor. All of the parts that touch you and your breast milk can be purchased brand-new and sterile.

15. How do I store expressed breast milk?

Depending on the pump you have, breast milk can be pumped directly into special breast milk freezer bags or into bottles designed for refrigerator or freezer storage. To thaw breast milk for serving, hold the bag or bottle containing the frozen milk under warm running water or use a bottle warmer, but do not microwave! Microwaving destroys the healthy infection-fighting antibodies in your milk as well as heats the milk unevenly, which could seriously burn a baby's mouth. If you know how much milk your baby is likely to drink the next day, take that amount of frozen breast milk from the freezer the night before and place it in the refrigerator to thaw. Be aware that you shouldn't refreeze thawed breast milk, so try to plan accordingly and only defrost what you think your baby will need.

So for how long is expressed breast milk good? Just remember what I call the rule of 4s. Freshly expressed milk can be stored as noted in the following list:

- Up to 4 hours at room temperature. Thawed breast milk should never be stored at room temperature.
- Up to 4 days in the refrigerator. This applies to freshly expressed breast milk, whereas previously frozen breast milk is only safely stored for 24 hours in the refrigerator.
- Up to 4 months in the freezer. If you have a stand-alone freezer (like a meat locker) it can be stored for up to 6 to 12 months. Keep the milk at the very back of the freezer where it is consistently coldest. If your ice cream and ice cubes are hard, it's cold enough.

Common Concerns

16. My baby falls asleep at my breast. What can I do to help him stay awake while eating?

Falling asleep while eating is very common, especially in the first few weeks. Nursing is very soothing to infants. That, combined with the warmth your baby feels being snuggled against your chest, is an ideal combination to put anyone to sleep. In addition, some babies will tend to fall asleep in the first few weeks of life when the flow of milk is slow, not necessarily because they have had enough to eat. If this is the case, gentle breast compression (use your opposite hand to hold your breast with the thumb on top and other fingers below) may help your baby get more milk and continue to nurse when he gets sleepy and his sucking slows down. It is important that your baby stay awake long enough to eat enough calories to gain weight and grow. Ideally he will finish a full feed, but during those first few weeks, this may be next to impossible each and every time you nurse him. Try stripping your baby down to only his diaper for nursing. Stroke his head, neck, or back, or tickle his feet as needed to keep him awake. Between breasts is a good time to burp him or change his diaper; better yet, have Daddy change it—a sure way to wake them both up.

 Call your pediatrician if your baby is so sleepy that you can't wake him to eat or if he has skipped 2 meals in a row.

DR. TANYA'S TIP
To Increase Milk Supply...

- Stay hydrated (keep a water bottle within reach while nursing).
- Eat a balanced diet (about 500 calories more than you ate before pregnancy...yummy!).
- Breastfeed regularly.
- Pump it up (pump an extra morning feed if you have time).
- Get enough sleep (or as much as possible).

While there is not enough medical evidence to support the use of fenugreek capsules, Mother's Milk Tea, barley, or oatmeal to increase milk supply, many moms swear that they really do work.

 Always ask your pediatrician before using any medications or herbal supplements to make sure they are safe and don't have unwanted side effects.

17. My nipples are so sore that I cry during feeds. Help!
Been there! Sore, cracked nipples, most often caused by improper latch and vigorous or prolonged sucking, can be
extremely painful and are the reason why some moms quit
nursing. Enlisting the advice of a lactation consultant at the
first sign of trouble, if not before, to learn proper latch and
positioning techniques along with good nipple hygiene can
usually prevent or resolve this irritating issue altogether. If
you are experiencing pain, here are some tips to help your
nipples heal and prevent further soreness.

- Even if you think your baby is latching on well, chances
  are your positioning may be slightly off. See Pediatric
  Point: Proper Positioning on page 26. If that doesn't
  help, call a lactation consultant ASAP!
- Allow your nipples to air-dry after you feed your baby or
  shower. Then apply a lanolin cream labeled as safe for
  you and baby.
- Express a few drops of breast milk, rub over your nipple,
  and allow to air-dry.
- Wear a cotton bra, loose-fitting top, or nipple shells, or
  even go bare when possible.
- Apply a cool compress or gel pads after nursing and a
  warm compress before nursing.
- Change nursing pads frequently.
- Try shorter feeds, or feed on one side at a time and give
  the other side a chance to heal.
- Continue breastfeeding!
- A neck and shoulder massage from Daddy may not help
  the pain, but it sure doesn't hurt.

Call your pediatrician or lactation consultant if these remedies do not help within 24 to 48 hours, the pain is getting worse, a burning pain is experienced later on in breastfeeding (could be a yeast infection), or your baby spits up blood-tinged milk (may come from your cracked nipples). Call your obstetrician if you develop increasing, persistent, or severe breast pain, fever, aches, and general flu-like symptoms. You may have a breast infection (mastitis) that requires treatment with an antibiotic.

PEDIATRIC POINT
Proper Positioning

Improper latch-on can cause pain and really interfere with breastfeeding. Here is a walk-through on proper latch straight from my own lactation consultant, Elisa Hirsch, RN, BSN, IBCLC.

Position your baby with her body facing yours and with her nose close to your nipple. Allow your baby's head to tilt back so she's looking up at you. Wait for her to open her mouth widely. When she does, bring her closer to you with her chin in very close to your breast. With your finger, guide your nipple into the top half of your baby's mouth. When your baby is positioned properly her chin will be against the breast and you'll see more areola (darker area) showing near your baby's nose than chin. When your nipple comes out of your baby's mouth it may look a bit longer, but the shape of the nipple should look the same as it was before the feed. A feeling of tugging is normal, but pain is a sign that you should ask for help.

18. My baby spits up often. Is this normal?

All babies spit up once in a while, but some babies spit up more frequently, leading moms to wonder if their newborn is allergic to something in the adult diet passing through the breast milk. In many instances, spit-up is not caused by an allergy but reflux, or a baby getting too much milk too quickly. Reflux is discussed in more detail in Chapter 4, but simply put, some of the milk that your baby drinks (along with stomach acids) manages to work its way back up from the stomach. If your baby seems to gulp and gasp, try taking her off the breast for a little rest or even a burp before putting her back on. Have a burp cloth handy to catch the milk that happens to spurt out. Giving smaller feeds more frequently, such as one breast instead of both at each feeding, and keeping your baby in an upright position for 10 to 15 minutes after a feed instead of laying her down, can also help. Despite your best efforts, the fact of the matter is that spitting up is often a part of newborn life. If this is the case, keep stacks of burp cloths everywhere and don't forget an extra change of clothes for baby (as well as you) when going out.

In some instances, your baby may develop an allergy to something that you are eating. The most common offenders are milk and soy products, but eggs, nuts, wheat, fish, shellfish, citrus, and others are also possibilities. Always talk to your physician before restricting your diet, as proper nutrition is essential for breastfeeding.

 If your baby's spit-up seems excessive, she seems very uncomfortable, or she has extreme crying or poor weight gain, call your pediatrician. In addition, if there is any diarrhea, blood in the stool, or vomiting, an allergy is more likely to be a potential culprit, so check with your pediatrician.

> ### PEDIATRIC POINT
> ### Excess Gas?
>
> Certain foods that make you gassy may also cause gas in your baby and make him uncomfortable. A few culprits include spicy dishes, broccoli, cauliflower, and beans.

19. I have a cold. Should I continue nursing?

Absolutely. Your breast milk can actually help protect your infant from catching your cold. Your body begins making antibodies as soon as you become infected. These protective antibodies are passed to your baby through your breast milk. Chances are that your baby was exposed to your illness before you even started feeling sick, so if you stop nursing there is an even greater chance that she will catch your cold. It's still a good idea to wash your hands before touching your baby, and try to avoid directly coughing or sneezing on her.

 If your doctor recommends that you stop nursing because of a serious illness, medication, or treatment that you need, talk to your pediatrician. There may be a way to continue feeding your baby your breast milk.

20. Can I have a glass of wine or a cup of coffee or take over-the-counter medications while I'm breastfeeding?

What goes in, must come out! A great deal of what you eat or drink will pass through to your breast milk and can potentially affect your baby.

You may be surprised to know that occasional moderate alcohol consumption is actually OK (the American Academy of Pediatrics even says so). The best time to have that glass of wine is right after you finish nursing or pumping and at least 2 hours before your next feed or pumping session. That way your body has as much time as possible to get rid of the alcohol and less will reach your baby.

While you don't have to quit caffeine cold turkey, it's worth pointing out that while caffeine may perk you up, it also may cause fussiness and wakefulness in some babies. It is therefore best to limit your overall intake of caffeine, whether your preference is coffee, tea, caffeinated soda, or even chocolate. Although some experts say that up to 3 cups a day may be fine, it's probably best to stick with the minimum you need.

When it comes to medications or herbal supplements, as always, you'll want to check with your baby's pediatrician before taking any. Also, make sure your own physician knows you are breastfeeding before any medication is prescribed for you. Luckily, most over-the-counter pain medications such as acetaminophen (Tylenol) and some cold medications (when taken in appropriate amounts) are safe while breastfeeding. It is important to note that any medication that dries up your secretions or nasal congestion (such as decongestants and antihistamines) may have the same effect on your breast milk, especially if taken regularly.

CHAPTER 3

Formula Feeds
"Bottle talk"

If you are unable to breastfeed or after careful consideration have decided that it isn't for you and your baby, there are many types of formulas for you to consider that will provide your baby with all of the nutrition needed to grow and develop. Plenty of Ivy League-bound students and successful venture capitalists were formula-fed as infants and keep up just fine with their breastfed counterparts.

What may be even more difficult than deciding whether to use infant formula is what formula to use and how to feed it to your little one. You may be bombarded with choices. Many have docosahexaenoic acid (DHA) and arachidonic acid (ARA), most have iron, and others are organic or have probiotics. In this chapter, I will attempt to make sense of the smorgasbord of infant formulas available.

Formula Facts

21. Formula...so many choices. Where do I start?

Ever wish there were a simple mathematical formula that would allow you to calculate which infant formula is best for your baby? Unfortunately, it's not that easy. The good news is that any major brand formula on the market should be fine and most babies do very well on the first one they are given. Your pediatrician can help you select an appropriate formula for your baby.

Here's the scoop on infant formula.

Main Types

- **Milk based:** This is recommended as the formula of choice for infants not receiving breast milk. Most infants grow and develop very well on milk-based formula.
- **Soy based:** Soy protein is used instead of cow milk protein and is naturally lactose free. Soy formula is a good alternative to milk-based formula for vegetarian families and some infants allergic or intolerant to milk-based formula.
- **Protein hydrolysate and elemental:** Often referred to as hypoallergenic formulas, they are made specifically for infants with a true allergy or severe intolerance to standard cow milk and soy protein-containing formulas. While it may be more easily digested, it is also significantly more expensive.

Additives

- **Iron:** Iron is vital for blood and brain development. Contrary to popular belief, iron in formula does not cause constipation. More importantly, low-iron formulas do not contain enough iron for a baby's growing needs.

- **DHA and ARA:** These are 2 fatty acids (lipids) that naturally occur in breast milk and are thought to be important in brain and eye development. DHA and ARA have now been added to many formulas.
- **Probiotics:** Similar to those found in yogurt with live bacteria cultures, probiotics have recently been added to some infant formula. Although the use of probiotics is advertised as leading to a healthier immune system and decreased infant illness, more studies need to be done on the risks and benefits.
- **Organic:** New on the market are organic formulas. They are certified to be pesticide, antibiotic and growth hormone free. Only time and research will tell if there is any medical benefit, but if buying organic is important to you, it is fine. Just make sure you buy a reputable brand to ensure that it contains everything your baby needs to grow and develop.

Preparations

- **Ready to feed:** As the name states, your baby can drink the formula as is. Although convenient for travel if you can't or don't want to carry water for mixing, the bottles are heavy to carry around and often more expensive.
- **Liquid concentrate:** Easy to mix—you simply add equal parts of the liquid formula and water, shake, and feed. Again, it is heavier to haul around in your baby bag and a slightly more expensive option than powder.

- **Powder:** This preparation is the most commonly used and least expensive option. Also, powder is fairly light to carry. The mixing ratio is 2 ounces of water for 1 scoop of powder formula. Simply shake or stir and then serve.

DR. TANYA'S TIP
Drinking On the Go

Premeasure scoops of powder formula into a dry bottle for storage in your baby bag. When it's time to feed, just add the appropriate amount of bottled water (2 ounces of water per 1 scoop of powder formula), shake, and serve. Room-temperature water is fine.

---

22. Should I boil the water I use to mix my baby's formula?

That depends on your local water supply. In most areas in the United States, regular tap water is fine, but in some areas, primarily those where well water is used, it may be recommended to boil tap water for 1 minute to sterilize it before using it to make formula. You can also buy bottled water.

In addition, you should determine whether there is fluoride in your area's water supply and talk to your pediatrician or pediatric dentist about your baby's fluoride needs. Although some fluoride is important for developing teeth that have not yet made their appearance above the gums, too much fluoride can cause problems, especially for babies younger than 6 months.

23. Do I need to warm the formula before giving it to my baby?

Room-temperature formula is fine for babies (even from day one) and easier for you. Although it's not necessary, if you would like to warm the formula (or your mother insists that you do), go ahead. Use a bottle warmer, run the bottle under warm running water, or let it sit in a pot of warm water. Do not microwave, as this can cause hot pockets in the formula that may inadvertently burn your baby. Always make sure to shake the bottle before testing the temperature (a few drops on your inner wrist works well) because some areas in the bottle may be warmer than others. As your baby gets older, transition to mixing your formula with room-temperature water. Remember that if your baby gets used to drinking warm formula, you will run into problems when you are out and don't have a way to warm the formula to the desired temperature. Even premature babies have been successfully fed refrigerated formula. It's all about what your baby gets used to.

PEDIATRIC POINT
Formula for Toddlers?

Toddler formulas are now available from a variety of formula companies. Made for 9- to 24-month-olds, these formulas do have extra vitamins and nutrients compared with regular whole milk. But are they really necessary? Reports have concluded that in many cases, they aren't. If your child is eating a balanced diet and growing and developing well, regular milk is sufficient for your child's needs after her first birthday.

Unexpected Upsets

24. My baby is fussy and gassy and spits up often. Should I switch formula?

Some babies are fussy and gassy and spit up more often than others. It's rarely dangerous, but it isn't exactly fun either. Many parents try different formulas in search of one that relieves their baby's symptoms. While such symptoms do not indicate a true allergy, in some cases they suggest an intolerance to a specific type of formula. While some babies seem to show a preference for a specific type or brand of formula, most babies do fine on the first formula they are given. For parents who are constantly switching on a quest for that one magic formula, when they eventually find it, often the reason is that their infant is older anyway and has outgrown the symptoms.

 While it is not dangerous to switch formula and can be tempting if you have a sample or coupon, it's always best to check with your pediatrician first.

25. How do I know if my baby is allergic to milk-based formula?

Signs of a true milk protein allergy are usually not subtle. You may see hives (blotchy red skin rash), eczema, facial swelling, vomiting, or trouble breathing. Another type of formula allergy may produce bloody diarrhea and poor weight gain. There are some babies, however, who may have more mild symptoms such as spitting up, fussiness, and changes in stool pattern. Always talk to your pediatrician if you are concerned that your baby may have a milk or other food allergy.

 If your baby experiences any trouble breathing, facial swelling, vomiting, or hives, call your pediatrician immediately. The doctor may recommend that your baby be given a soy-based or hypoallergenic formula.

PEDIATRIC POINT
Baby Bottle Tooth Decay

Please don't put your baby to bed with a bottle. Falling asleep while drinking milk or juice can lead to cavities because the liquid pools around the teeth and provides a place for bacteria to grow. In addition to being bad for baby teeth, there can also be damage to future permanent teeth. Also, falling asleep while drinking increases your baby's chance of ear infections. Bottle propping (when a bottle is propped up to allow a child to drink without a parent holding it) is just as bad and may also lead to choking as the milk continues to flow out. Don't start an unnecessary feeding habit that often leads to a bad sleeping habit—both difficult to break.

CHAPTER 4

Solids, Milk, and Other Feeding Issues

"À la carte"

What kind of pediatrician and parent would I be if I didn't take this opportunity to stress the importance of proper nutrition? As a parent, you are your child's best role model when it comes to eating healthy. Kids like to eat what they see their parents eating. And if you get excited about a particular item, they will too. That's how I got my toddler to eat broccoli every night for dinner. I'm not going to tell you that it's easy. After his first grilled cheese sandwich, he was hooked and that was all he wanted. So mysteriously, all of the bread and cheese in the house disappeared for a week until he forgot about it. If the only choices available are healthy ones, most older infants and toddlers will take to eating healthier options and learn to love them. Would you believe that I have toddlers in my practice that eat high-fiber cereal with raisins and nonfat milk and drink a cup of water for breakfast almost every day?

In the Beginning

26. Should I give my baby water?

Newborn

There is no need to give any water, sugar water, electrolyte solutions (such as Pedialyte, Enfalyte, or LiquiLyte), or juice to newborns unless directed by your pediatrician. Breast milk or formula is all your baby needs.

Infant

Once your infant starts solids, around 4 to 6 months of age, you can start introducing water at mealtimes. Getting your infant used to the taste of water (instead of sweet beverages) will create a healthy habit for life.

27. How can I be sure that my newborn is getting enough to eat?

In addition to following how much and how often your baby eats, it is helpful to track his weight as well as how much he pees and poops. During the first 2 weeks of life, breastfed babies should feed 8 to 12 times a day, about 15 to 20 minutes on each breast. Formula-fed babies will typically drink approximately 1 or 2 ounces every 3 to 4 hours (the amount at each feed will increase after the first week or two). Your pediatrician will closely follow your baby's weight, as newborns may lose up to 10% of their birth weight in the first week. By the end of the second week, however, they usually gain it back. After that, babies usually gain about an ounce a day. Most babies double their birth weight by 5 or 6 months of age and triple it by 1 year.

In the first week, a good way to determine if enough is going in is to keep track of what is coming out.

Day of Life	Wet Diapers (Urine)	Dirty Diapers (Stool)
1	1 or more	1 or more
2	3 or more	2 or more
3	4 or more	3 or more
4	5 or more	3 or more

For the next few weeks, your baby should have about 5 wet and 3 dirty diapers a day. Don't forget that many times a diaper has urine and stool mixed together.

 Let your pediatrician know if your baby is having fewer wet and dirty diapers than listed in the Table or has a change in his usual pattern.

FUN FACT
Baby Burps

Most babies need burping for the first few months to help get rid of swallowed air. Of course you won't always be able to get a burp. If you've been trying for 5 minutes and he seems comfortable, it's OK to give up. Some babies feel better having a burp halfway through a feed, while others are fine waiting until the full feeding is over. Following are several different burping techniques:

1. Sit baby on your lap and lean his weight slightly forward against one of your hands.
2. Drape him over your shoulder.
3. Lay him tummy-side down over your lap. With your other hand, gently pat and rub his back.

28. My baby spits up all the time. Is this normal? When should I worry?

Spit-up happens! For some babies it happens often. Most of the time it looks just like the milk they drink and occurs soon after feeding. Other times it is curdled like old milk or smelly like vomit and can occur an hour or two after a feed. Spit-up is caused by taking too much volume in at once or reflux (see question #29 on the next page). It should not be forceful, although if you are holding your baby up on your shoulder, it may shoot over your shoulder and down your back (if you're lucky it will miss your hair!). So buy burp cloths by the dozens and keep them everywhere. (As an aside, formula spit-up often stains more than breast milk spit-up, so protect yourself accordingly.) Spitting up also shouldn't cause a great deal of discomfort for your baby. In fact, your baby may feel better after a good spit-up. As she gets older, the spitting up will improve and usually resolves by 6 to 12 months of age.

 Call your doctor if the spit-up seems forceful (shoots across the room), your baby seems to be in pain, or you notice any blood or greenish color in the spit-up or any increase in frequency or intensity of the spit-up. Also call if her belly looks swollen or distended or feels hard. In addition, let your pediatrician know if you notice that your baby doesn't seem to be gaining weight or is having fewer wet and dirty diapers, as these may be signs that not enough of what she eats is staying down.

29. What is *reflux?* I see this word in a lot of parenting magazines.

Reflux is the name used for spitting up caused by stomach contents going the wrong way out of the stomach. It is very common in babies because the feeding tube (esophagus) is short and the muscle at the bottom of the feeding tube and top of the stomach is relaxed and floppy. This allows food in the stomach to more easily come back up and out the mouth. Hence the spit-up! In addition to the spit-up, reflux can sometimes cause such symptoms as pain or discomfort. As long as a baby with reflux is eating well and gaining weight normally and isn't too uncomfortable, usually no treatment is needed. The feeding tube will lengthen and the muscle will naturally tighten as he grows so the reflux usually resolves by about 1 year of age. In the meantime, giving smaller, more frequent feeds and holding him upright for 10 to 15 minutes after a feed will help. Your pediatrician may also recommend changing the consistency of his formula or breast milk (using a thicker formula or adding a small amount of rice cereal).

 If your baby frequently spits up or has any of the following symptoms, talk to your pediatrician. Medication or other tests and treatment options may be necessary.

- Your baby is not feeding well or is not gaining weight appropriately.
- Your baby develops any respiratory symptoms like coughing, choking, or wheezing.
- Your baby seems uncomfortable, cries, or arches after a feed (may not always spit up).
- The spit-up is projectile (literally shoots across the room).

Solids and Such

30. When can I start solids?

The American Academy of Pediatrics and most pediatricians recommend starting solids at 4 to 6 months, depending on when your infant is ready.

So how do you know when your infant is ready? All babies grow and develop at slightly different rates, and although some cultures start solids in the first few months with no apparent harmful effects, this isn't generally recommended because your infant really isn't developmentally ready for solid food yet.

First, she has to have good head control, which most infants demonstrate in the 4- to 6-month age range. In addition, she needs to be able to move the food with her tongue from the front to the back of her mouth, also something that occurs from 4 to 6 months. If you put a small amount of rice cereal on her tongue and she pushes it out of her mouth (tongue thrust reflex), she may not be developmentally ready for solid food. But if she is drinking more than 36 ounces a day, it's probably time for a bit of solid nutrition. Another sign you will begin to notice around this age is that she may pull away from the breast and bottle, looking around for other interesting things to do (or eventually eat). She may also watch you intently as you eat.

As long as your baby is at least 4 months old and meeting most of these criteria, go ahead and talk to your pediatrician about trying solids. If she spits the food out, simply wait a few days and try again.

Remember to touch base with your pediatrician at the 4-month checkup to get advice on starting solid food.

31. Cereal, fruits, veggies, or meat—what order is best? How do I introduce solids?

There are no strict guidelines anymore on the order in which solids should be introduced. While most parents are excited to feed their infants a wide variety of foods immediately, I like to take a slower approach. What's the hurry? Your infant has his entire life to eat. Because most parents I see in my office ask me to point them in some direction, here are some basic guidelines that can be altered by you, your infant, or your pediatrician.

With most infants I prefer to try rice cereal first because the taste is fairly mild and acceptable to most infants. In addition, it is fortified with iron and nutrients and the chance of an allergy to rice cereal is extremely low. Prepare the cereal using breast milk, formula, or water. Initially make it a soup-like consistency so it runs right off the spoon. If your infant takes it, you can make it slightly thicker over time. At first your infant may only take half of a baby spoonful once or twice a day, but will probably increase quickly to a tablespoon amount (still fed with a tiny baby spoon) twice a day.

After your infant has successfully taken rice cereal for at least 4 days, you can try oatmeal or barley cereal or you can go straight to veggies or fruits. Always wait at least 4 days before introducing a new food item, just in case your infant has an allergic reaction. That way you'll be more likely to know which food caused the problem. Food allergies are more common in children with a family history of food allergies or other allergic conditions such as asthma, hay fever, or eczema.

For veggies and fruits, I suggest starting with stage 1 (or a very pureed consistency if homemade) orange veggies (such as carrots and sweet potato), then yellow veggies (squash, for example), and later green veggies (such as peas and green beans). Peas and green beans are in the legume family (like peanuts) so they have a slight risk of allergic reaction. Once your infant loves his veggies, try starting a fruit, such as pears or apples (still stage 1, very pureed consistency).

What time should your baby be fed? Initially, whatever time works into your daily routine (if you don't have a routine yet, I suggest you start one). I fed my first son oatmeal with a veggie or fruit mid-morning and rice cereal with a veggie for dinner for a month or two before moving to 3 meals a day. Within a few months, most infants will eat 3 meals a day, ideally with the rest of the family, which should ultimately be your goal.

When do you move to stage 2 baby foods (slightly chunkier texture than stage 1)? Whenever your child has exhausted the stage 1 options and you think he can handle slightly more texture. If you're not sure he's ready, just give it a try and if he doesn't take it, back up and try again next week. Once on stage 2, there are several meats that you can add into his diet. If you're making your own, try pureeing or mashing the chicken or turkey to a lumpy pureed consistency.

Food allergies cause symptoms such as facial swelling, rash or hives, vomiting, diarrhea, wheezing, or trouble breathing. Call your doctor right away if you notice any of these symptoms. If your infant is having trouble breathing, call 911.

32. Are there any foods in particular to avoid?

- **Honey:** *NEVER give a baby younger than 1 year honey* because of the risk of infant botulism, a deadly disease. Babies, unlike older children and adults, don't have the ability to fight the botulinum toxin contained in honey.
- **Choking hazards:** Whole nuts, grapes, popcorn, hot dogs, and raw carrots are serious choking hazards, so keep these and other small or hard foods away from infants and toddlers.
- **Food allergy:** It was previously recommended to hold off on giving highly allergenic foods such as egg whites, shellfish, peanuts, and tree nuts until after 2 or even 3 years of age, depending on a child's family history of allergies. Although further studies need to be done, there is little evidence that holding off on introducing such foods to an infant who shows no sign of allergic disease (such as eczema) has any effect on whether the child will develop allergies to these foods. Your pediatrician may have specific recommendations for introducing foods associated with allergy.

Food allergies are more common in children with a family history of food allergies, asthma, hay fever, and eczema. If your child falls into this category, talk to your pediatrician about when the best time is to introduce such foods to your child.

33. Should I worry about my toddler's picky eating habits?

Between 1 and 5 years of age, children typically experience a slowing of weight gain. They aren't growing as fast as they were in the first year of life. That means it's normal for children to start eating less at around 12 to 18 months. It may seem like they are picky or have a poor appetite. Many will refuse to try new foods or suddenly reject entire food groups that they previously liked. Or your child may want the same food over and over and over…. My mom says that I would only eat food with raisins in it until I was 3 years old! Surprisingly, picky eating typically won't lead to poor health or nutritional deficiencies.

Don't force your child to eat! Mealtime will become the worst time of the day if you do. Sometimes the need for control rather than being picky causes the problem, so let your child be in charge of what and how much she eats—at least to a certain extent—by offering 2 choices of nutritious meals and snacks.

A child's likes and dislikes may change day-to-day or month-to-month. Many children grow well by only eating foods of their favorite color, so be creative because almost every color has some healthy options.

Remember that a toddler's portion size is about one third of an adult serving. As a rough guideline for a person of any age, an appropriate portion size is usually about the size of that person's palm. It's also not unusual for children to have one good meal, one fair meal, and one poor meal a day—all of which can ultimately average out to a fairly decent amount. Offer healthy food and let your child eat as much (or as little) as she wants. This will help avoid unnecessary battles over food.

If you find yourself still struggling with a picky eater or are simply craving more advice, *Food Fights: Winning the Nutritional Challenges of Parenthood Armed With Insight, Humor, and a Bottle of Ketchup* by Laura A. Jana, MD, FAAP, and Jennifer Shu, MD, FAAP, has helped many parents bring "peas and harmony" to the family table.

 When should you worry? Call your pediatrician if you are concerned about your child's growth or weight gain, and don't forget to enlist the doctor's help in your overall approach to your child's nutrition.

FUN FACT
Trial by the Dozens

Studies show that it can take about a dozen tries of a new food item for your child to like it! Keep this in mind as you continue placing those green veggies on your toddler's tray and show her that you like them too…mmm! Eventually she will start eating them and may grow to like them as well. Studies show the more fruits and veggies eaten as a child, the more fruits and veggies children are likely to eat when they get older.

PEDIATRIC POINT
Toddler Vitamins

The American Academy of Pediatrics recommends that all children receive 400 IU of vitamin D every day, which can be found in many over-the-counter children's vitamins. Unless your child is drinking 32 oz a day of vitamin D–fortified milk, consider giving your toddler a vitamin supplement. Remember to store the vitamins (as well as all medications and supplements) out of your child's reach.

Milk (and Other Liquid) Matters

34. How and when do I transition from bottle to cup?

Infant

Introduce the sippy or straw cup around 6 to 9 months of age. Your infant may not take to it immediately, but keep trying. You can start with water to avoid messy spills, but very soon offer breast milk or formula in a cup as well. Once your child has mastered the sippy or straw cup, you can begin to wean him from the bottle with a goal of having him drinking completely out of a cup by 12 to 15 months of age.

Toddler

If your child is older than 1 year, the transition from bottle to cup can be more challenging, especially if he considers the bottle a security or comfort object. You can try gradually weaning the bottle, but often after around 15 months of age, it's best to choose a day, gather up all the bottles, and give them away. If your child is old enough to understand, you can warn him the day before and explain that you are giving the bottles to a younger baby who needs them. He may scream and even refuse to drink for a day or two (don't worry, in this short time he won't dehydrate himself), but he'll quickly forget and soon take to the sippy or straw cup. Your ultimate goals: by 18 months, he should be off the bottle, and by 2 or 3 years of age, he should be off the sippy cup and drinking from a regular cup.

DR. TANYA'S TIP
Cup That Milk

I see too many parents who only give milk in the bottle and save the sippy cup for water and juice. Then when it comes time to get rid of the bottle, their child stops drinking milk. But you can avoid this problem. Once you've introduced a sippy or straw cup (around 6 to 9 months), put breast milk or formula in it. That way your infant will get used to drinking milk from something other than a breast or bottle. At 1 year of age when you start whole or reduced-fat milk, your child will better accept it in a cup and it will make the transition to milk and the weaning off the bottle much easier.

35. When can I give my baby regular milk and how do I introduce it?

At 1 year of age and in a cup. If your baby is still nursing, you can offer regular milk in a cup and wean from breast-feeding as you desire. If she is on formula, just switch to regular whole milk. Many 1-year-olds will do fine with the abrupt transition, but if you or she prefer, you can mix the formula and whole milk to slowly transition her to the new, cold taste in a few days. Ideally your child will drink cold milk straight from the refrigerator in a cup. But if she is currently hooked on a bottle, you can switch her to the taste of regular milk in the bottle first, then a few weeks later, get rid of the bottle and use a cup.

It was previously recommended that all 1- to 2-year-olds receive whole milk. Experts felt that extra fat was needed for brain development and growth at that age. More recently, because of the increase in childhood obesity and the high-fat diet that many toddlers eat, 2% milk was also deemed fine for this age group. If your toddler is over-weight or there is a family history of obesity, heart disease, or high cholesterol, talk to your pediatrician about giving your toddler 2% instead of whole milk at 1 year of age. For other toddlers, I often stick with whole milk at least until 18 months and then, depending on how they are growing and what else they are eating, switch to 2% milk by 2 years of age. As part of a low-fat, balanced diet, after 2 years of age, most kids (and parents as well) should make their way to nonfat milk. Nonfat milk has the exact same calcium and nutrients as 1%, 2%, and regular milk, but with each percent there is just extra fat (think of pats of butter) stirred in.

36. One of my toddlers won't eat but loves milk. The other refuses milk. How much is too much and how little is OK?

Many kiddos don't eat because they fill up on liquid calories. Milk (especially if whole or 2%) can be very filling, so it's no wonder that he isn't hungry for food. Limit his milk to 16 ounces a day. Serve water with meals and offer milk after he finishes his food. This way he won't fill up on the milk first.

In most cases, 2 or 3 servings a day of calcium-rich food is all that your child needs. Toddlers require about 500 mg of calcium daily and can meet these needs from drinking about 2 servings (16 ounces or 2 cups) of milk. (Each cup of milk contains about 300 mg of calcium.) If your child refuses milk, offer 2 to 3 servings of other calcium-rich options like yogurt, cheese, green veggies, or orange juice with added calcium.

37. When can I give my child fruit juice?

It's actually best if you don't. Your infant or toddler does not need juice. Although 100% fruit juice may contain some useful vitamins, juice often ends up being extra sugar and calories that your child doesn't need. Plus, juice doesn't have the valuable fiber found in fruit. One of the best things you can do for your child's future nutritional health is to get your infant used to drinking water. How many adults do you know who don't like plain water? It's often because they didn't get used to the taste when they were young. Even watered-down juice on a regular basis can get your child in the habit of wanting sweet-tasting beverages. It's best to stick with water and milk whenever possible. If you do choose to give your child juice, keep it under 4 to 6 ounces a day. Treat sweet-tasting drinks like you would a dessert—on special occasions, let your toddler choose juice or another sweet treat such as cake. You might be surprised at his choice.

An exception to this recommendation is if your baby is constipated. In such cases, your pediatrician may recommend small amounts of prune, apple, or pear juice along with a high-fiber diet to help with this problem. See constipation questions #39 and #40 on pages 57 through 59 for more information.

CHAPTER 5

Pooping

"It's all about the poop."

Whether or not we like to admit it, a good portion of the first few years of parenting is all about the poop. It began with that first dark, thick, sticky dirty diaper you changed in the hospital and progresses into teaching your child how to get the poop in the potty. There are many colors, the consistency and frequency vary, and oh how lovely they smell. Poop is definitely on the list of most common topics parents like to call me about. They often worry it's too hard, too soft, too much, not enough, or the "wrong" color. It's rarely just right. I can't tell you how many poop presents, wrapped in diapers, plastic bags, or even plastic containers, I've been asked to look at. To help you sort out what's right and what might warrant a call to your pediatrician, here's more than you ever thought you'd want to know about poop.

Normal Poop

38. What should the poop look like?

Newborn

While your newborn may already resemble you, her stool won't. Baby poop comes in a wide variety of colors, consistencies, and frequencies. During the first 24 hours of life, stools are usually thick, sticky, and brownish-black in color—meconium. After the first few days and over the course of the first few weeks, the stools of breastfed babies lighten in color from black to brown to green to yellow. They also change consistency from sticky to seedy to cottage cheese-like to even looser. In contrast, formula-fed babies often have stools that are thicker in consistency and light brown in color.

Infant

As infants grow, generally speaking, their stool pattern slows down. Some may poop many times a day, while others poop every few days. The color may range from yellow to brown, with a green one thrown in every so often for added color.

Toddler

With an increase in solid food intake, toddler stools typically look (and smell) more like adult stools. Some variation in color and consistency is normal, often depending on what children eat and drink. If you find a neon green surprise in your toddler's diaper, it may be the dye in the juice that your toddler is drinking—just one more reason to give water instead!

Although variation in stool color is normal, some colors do warrant further investigation. If your child starts to have stools that are black after the first few days of life, red or bloody, white, chalky, or clay colored, call your pediatrician and bring in a stool sample to be checked out.

Constipation

39. My baby hasn't pooped for 3 days. What should I do?

Newborn

Believe it or not, this is one of the more common questions pediatricians hear. In the first few weeks of life, your newborn really should poop every day; if not, let your pediatrician know. Although less frequent pooping can be normal, it's possible that he isn't drinking enough to produce frequent poop. Rarely, there could be something hindering the stool from coming out, such as a condition called Hirschsprung disease, in which the end of the intestines or anus isn't working properly.

After demonstrating that all of his parts are working well—at least one stool before going home from the hospital and a few good weeks of eating and pooping regularly—it is normal for a breastfed baby to stool anywhere from roughly once every 5 days up to 11 times a day. Around 2 months of age, your baby may change his pooping pattern, usually becoming less frequent. Formula-fed babies tend to poop less often than breastfed babies. As long as your baby is acting fine and drinking enough breast milk or formula, and the stool isn't too hard, just wait. He will eventually poop.

Infant

Generally speaking, the answer is…don't worry! Infants usually poop less often than newborns and some may only go once a week (how nice for those few lucky parents). In addition, they may push, grunt, and strain—all in the name of a poop. Their face may also turn as red as a tomato. As long as what comes out is soft, these behaviors are fine. So if your infant is drinking and eating (if already on solid food) well and the stool isn't too hard, give him some time to let it come out. If the stool is large and hard or looks like small rocks, or if he hasn't gone for a few days and is very uncomfortable, try giving him an ounce or two of water or prune juice to help soften the stool and make it easier for him to push out.

Call your pediatrician if you have any concerns, your child's belly seems to be swollen or distended, or he starts vomiting, develops a fever, or is tired and not interested in feeding. If your otherwise healthy newborn isn't stooling at least once a day in the first few weeks of life, or after that if it's been an entire week without poop, let your pediatrician know.

DR. TANYA'S TIP
Palatable Prunes

If your constipated baby won't drink the prune juice or water, mix it with some breast milk or formula and he'll be more likely to take it. Once your infant is eating solid food, try stage 1 baby prunes. Some babies do well with a little prune every morning for breakfast. Check in with your pediatrician to make sure nothing else is needed.

---

40. My toddler has a tendency to become constipated. What can I give her to soften her stool?

Constipation is common in toddlers and can cause endless problems. If it hurts, they won't go. So they hold it in, which makes it hurt even more. It also can really interfere with potty training (see question #96, pages 147–149). Correcting and preventing constipation are very important no matter what age your kids (or you) are. There are 5 fruits and 4 juices that are natural laxatives.

- Fruits: prunes, plums, cherries, apricots, and grapes
- Juices: prune juice, apple juice, apricot nectar, and pear nectar

I find that prune juice seems to work the best. If your child won't drink prune juice (make sure you tell her how yummy it is), mix one part prune juice with two parts apple juice. Apple juice works too, but some kids need 2 to 3 cups a day (not watered down), which is a lot of sugar. Drinking plenty of water every day will help as well.

Vegetables like cauliflower and broccoli have natural fiber that helps keep children regular. Be sure to include fiber in your family's daily diet. When making pancakes, waffles, or oatmeal, add extra oat bran to the mix. Some frozen waffles come with oat bran too. Choose breakfast cereal and bread with at least 3 grams of fiber per serving. Read labels and you'll be surprised how many good-tasting options there are. Whole wheat bread and tortillas are good choices as well. Look for high-fiber wafers or crackers—2 of these a day keep many constipated preschoolers regular. If dietary changes aren't working well enough, talk to your pediatrician about a plan to help soften your toddler's stools. Your child may benefit from a special diet or trying an over-the-counter medication.

Diarrhea

41. Why does my child get horrible diarrhea almost every winter?

Rotavirus is the most common infectious cause of diarrhea in children, although several other viruses are to blame as well. It occurs most often during the winter months; many parents refer to this type of infection as the "stomach flu." The typical course is fever and vomiting for a few days often followed by green, foul-smelling, watery diarrhea for a week or sometimes even longer. Older children and adults (who have stronger immune systems) may get lucky and only have mild symptoms, but many younger children can have serious vomiting and diarrhea. Small children in particular are more likely to be hospitalized from dehydration caused by rotavirus. It can spread like wildfire throughout child care centers and preschools where children are in close contact with each other, leading to increased risk of spreading and sharing germs. How do you reduce your family's chances of catching it? Wash your hands and teach your children to as well. Luckily, there is also now a vaccine typically given at the 2-, 4-, and 6-month well-child visits to help prevent infants from catching rotavirus.

42. What should I give my child when he has diarrhea?

The most important thing is to give plenty of liquids. This is often easier said than done, especially when everything is coming out the other end so quickly. If your child is also vomiting, keeping him hydrated can be even more challenging (see question #47, page 69).

Newborn

Newborns with diarrhea can easily get dehydrated, so it's particularly important to call your pediatrician to discuss what to do and determine the cause of the diarrhea. Continue breast milk or formula unless your doctor directs you to stop. The pediatrician may recommend increasing your baby's fluid intake, giving an oral rehydration fluid (such as Pedialyte, Enfalyte, or LiquiLyte), or changing your baby's formula until the diarrhea slows down. Your doctor may also want to examine and weigh your newborn every day or every few days to make sure he isn't losing weight.

Infant

In addition to the newborn advice, if your infant is already taking solid food, he may not feel like much of it while he is sick. That's OK as long as he continues drinking fluids. When he does feel like eating, start simple with rice cereal and then slowly advance his diet as tolerated. Avoid juice if possible as this may make the diarrhea worse. Because the ultimate goal is to stay hydrated, if juice is absolutely the only thing that your infant will drink, try a juice with lower sugar content and water it down if you can.

Toddler

If regular milk seems to make the diarrhea worse, you may want to try lactose-free milk for a few days. Electrolyte replacement drinks (such as Pedialyte, Enfalyte, or LiquiLyte) can help keep kids hydrated. Avoid sugary beverages and juice because they will worsen the diarrhea. However, if you have a strong-willed toddler (as many are), anything he wants to drink is better than nothing in the name of keeping him hydrated. A regular diet is fine if your toddler desires it, but certain foods such as bread, rice, mashed potatoes, bananas, or applesauce may be easier initially on an upset stomach and may help slow the diarrhea.

For all ages: In addition to the hassle of managing diarrhea, help prevent an irritating and potentially painful diaper rash by coating your little one's bottom at every diaper change with a diaper cream containing zinc oxide. Despite your best efforts, a rash may still develop. If this is the case, continue to keep your child's bottom well covered with a protective layer of diaper cream and refer to question #72 on page 110 for further advice.

Call your doctor if your child refuses to drink fluids, the diarrhea contains blood or excessive mucus, your child has fewer wet diapers than usual, there is associated vomiting or fever, the diarrhea lasts for more than 1 week, or there are more than 8 stools per day.

43. After a few days on an antibiotic for an ear infection, my child started having loose stools. Is this an allergy? Should I stop the medicine?

This is not an allergic reaction to the medicine. Diarrhea and mild abdominal pain are two of the most common side effects of antibiotics. In addition, the loose stools may just be part of the original illness. As long as you keep your child hydrated by giving plenty of fluids, the loose stools shouldn't cause any harm (although you may have to treat a diaper rash). The diarrhea will likely stop soon after the antibiotic course is completed and the illness is over. Do not stop the antibiotic without calling your pediatrician first. Some physicians now suggest giving yogurt with live cultures or probiotics to help replace the good gut bacteria that antibiotics can wipe out.

 Call your pediatrician if there is any vomiting, blood in the stool, or more than 8 loose stools a day or the diarrhea persists after the medication is stopped. In addition, if a fever persists for more than 2 to 3 days after starting antibiotics, see your pediatrician to check if the initial infection is resolving or there needs to be a change in the treatment plan.

CHAPTER 6

Stomachaches and Vomiting

"Mommy, my tummy hurts..."

There's nothing quite as distinct as the smell of my office after a child with the stomach flu has visited. Fortunately, not all stomachaches are associated with the upheaval of stomach contents. In fact, complaints of tummy pain are fairly common from toddler age on up. Differentiating between a complaint that is serious or one that is just due to too many snacks can be challenging, especially when there are tears involved. Although complaints of pain from your child should not be taken lightly, this chapter will provide some basic guidelines to help you figure out when you should worry and when you can relax.

Tummy Troubles

44. My toddler often complains of a tummy ache. It comes and goes, but the pain is not severe. What should I do?

As long as the pain isn't severe, worsening, or interfering with activity, you can take a moment to assess the situation. There are several questions that your pediatrician may ask, so it can be quite helpful to gather the information ahead of time to help figure out what's causing the pain.

- How long has the pain been present? Has it been days, weeks, or months?
- How bad is the pain? Does your child cry?
- Where is the pain? Around the belly button, or lower right belly?
- How long does the pain last? Does anything seem to make it better or worse?
- Any fever, vomiting, or diarrhea?
- Does the pain wake her up at night or interfere with activity?
- Does it happen only on preschool days, or a particular time of day?
- How is her appetite?
- Is it related to any specific food or drink such as milk products? Or is it better or worse after she eats?
- Is she potty trained? Does the pain occur only when she needs to poop?
- Does she poop every day? Is the stool hard or soft? Is it big or small? Is there any blood in the stool?
- Any recent social or family stress or change in environment?

- Any family history of stomach or intestinal diseases or issues?
- Any recent travel or exposure to pets?

These are some of the many questions that your pediatrician may ask when you call. It is often useful to keep a diary for the days leading up to the office visit (and sometimes even longer) and bring this to your appointment. The diary should include what your child eats and drinks, when the pain occurs, what she is doing at the time the pain occurs, how long it lasts, and most importantly, how often she poops and what it looks like. Also let the office know exactly why you are coming in (eg, stomachaches on and off for 3 months) so they can schedule extra time if needed for the appointment.

PEDIATRIC POINT
Soothing Stomach Cramps

There is no perfect way to help soothe a crampy tummy. Some parents find that simethicone (such as in Mylicon or other infant gas drops) may help their gassy baby. For older infants and toddlers, a warm bath will bring some relief. What caused the tummy ache? It may be gas, constipation, or a bit of an upset stomach. It also may be the first sign of a developing stomach virus (sometimes called the stomach flu), which means that vomiting and diarrhea will usually follow.

 Consult your doctor if the symptoms persist or are severe or if your child develops a fever, doesn't want to eat or drink, or isn't acting well.

45. My child has a bad stomachache. When should I worry?

Infant

Toddler

Infants and toddlers often can't tell you that their tummy hurts, so it can take some detective work on your part to figure out when you really need to call and have your child evaluated. The following signs and symptoms should be taken seriously because they may indicate a more pressing medical issue.

Call your pediatrician or schedule an appointment right away if any of the following is true:

- Your child looks sick.
- Pain is severe (especially in the lower right side).
- Pain is worsening.
- Pain is constant for more than 2 hours.
- Swollen or distended and tender belly.
- No interest in eating favorite food.
- Persistent vomiting.
- Persistent diarrhea.
- Bloody, dark, or grape jelly-looking poop.
- Can't jump up and down without pain (referring to toddlers, of course).
- Can't walk or walks hunched over (again, only applies to toddlers).

46. How do I know if the tummy ache is appendicitis?

Even doctors sometimes have a tough time diagnosing appendicitis, especially in young children, which is one of the reasons why a stomachache associated with any of the symptoms listed in the previous question should be evaluated right away. Typically, the signs and symptoms of appendicitis are tummy pain that starts around the belly button and over several hours moves to the lower right part of the belly. A child will cry or say it hurts when that area is pushed on. In addition, a child may have a fever, vomit, and not want to eat a favorite food if offered. Asking a toddler to jump can provide another clue. If it's appendicitis, most people—toddlers and adults alike—won't jump because it hurts when they do.

 Infants and toddlers with appendicitis don't always show the expected signs and symptoms, especially if they are younger than 2 years. Call your pediatrician if your child has any of the symptoms listed in question #45 on the previous page or if you are concerned about appendicitis. The doctor will need to examine your child and may order some tests including an ultrasound or computed tomography (CT) scan to look for appendicitis.

Vomiting and Dehydration

47. What do I give my child when he is vomiting?

Newborn

More often than not, what may seem to be newborn vomiting is actually just a lot of spit-up from taking too much in too quickly or reflux (see questions #28 and #29 on pages 42 and 43). However, true vomiting in a newborn does need to be evaluated, as it could be a sign of something more serious or lead to significant dehydration. Your pediatrician may recommend giving a little less volume at the next feed to see if it stays down. However, if the vomiting persists, this warrants a trip to your pediatrician's office or even the emergency department if the office is closed.

If the vomit becomes projectile (shoots a few feet across the room), is forceful, happens more than a few times, or occurs after 2 or more feedings in a row, that's a good reason to call the pediatrician. In addition, if the vomit contains any bright red blood or dark brown "coffee ground" material or you have any questions or concerns, call your pediatrician immediately or go to the emergency department.

Infant

Toddler

When a child is actively vomiting, it's best to hold off on giving anything. Once the vomiting seems to have stopped, try giving very small amounts of clear fluids frequently. Start with 1 teaspoon every 10 minutes; if that stays down for an hour or so you can slowly increase. Your pediatrician may recommend that you start with a clear electrolyte solution (such as Pedialyte, Enfalyte, or LiquiLyte). After several hours without further vomiting, your pediatrician may advise that you return to small amounts of milk (breast milk, formula, or regular milk) or whatever your child likes to drink for a few feeds before increasing slowly to the usual amounts. Many parents make the mistake of letting their thirsty child drink a few ounces at once, but with an uneasy stomach it will all come back up. It's best to avoid solids and stick with liquids for several hours after the vomiting has subsided. When you do introduce solids, go very slowly. Start small and simple, such as giving one spoonful of rice cereal or one cracker, and then wait about 30 minutes to see what happens.

 Call the doctor if your infant or toddler is unable to keep down even small amounts of fluids, vomiting persists for more than a few hours, there is any bright red blood or dark brown "coffee ground" material in the vomit, or your child has any signs of dehydration (see question #48, page 72).

DR. TANYA'S TIP
Recipe for Keeping Fluids Down

To avoid ending up in the hospital with intravenous fluids, consider this recipe for toddlers. If vomiting occurs, back up a step. If vomiting continues, it's important to call your pediatrician or go to the emergency department. With infants, it's best to touch base with your pediatrician before trying this or any other hydration plan. As with all recipes (even from grandma's kitchen), there may be similar versions that yield good results. Ultimately, the goal is to start small and increase as tolerated to keep down 4 to 8 ounces (oz) over several hours.

Hour 1: Nothing.
Hour 2: 1 tsp clear electrolyte solution every 10 minutes.
Hour 3: 2 tsp clear electrolyte solution every 15 minutes.
Hour 4: 0.5 oz clear electrolyte solution every 20 minutes.
Hour 5: 1 oz clear electrolyte solution every 30 minutes.
Hour 6: Very slowly resume normal fluids. (Formula or milk is usually fine.)

48. When do I need to worry about dehydration?

Dehydration is always a concern with sick children. Especially when infants and young children are vomiting, with or without diarrhea, they can easily and quickly become dehydrated. To prevent dehydration when your child is not feeling well, give small amounts of fluids frequently—as long as she can keep it down.

Newborns can become dehydrated very quickly. Don't wait until the signs of dehydration (as listed below for infants and toddlers) are present. If a newborn is vomiting, drinking less than usual, or having fewer wet or dirty diapers, call your pediatrician.

Newborn

Infant

Toddler

A call to the pediatrician should be made if a child is not keeping even small amounts of fluids down, vomiting persists for more than a few hours, diarrhea persists for more than a few days, or there are any signs of dehydration such as fewer wet diapers, lack of energy, no tears, dry lips and tongue, a sunken fontanelle (the soft spot on top of the head), irritability, or sunken eyes.

CHAPTER 7

Fever

"Feeling hot, hot, hot"

Many parents panic when their child feels warm. "Could it be? Oh no, it's a fever! Call the doctor!" A fever isn't a disease itself—just a symptom, or rather a byproduct of an illness. If your newborn is younger than 3 months, it may be appropriate to worry and definitely is appropriate to call your pediatrician—no matter what the time. As long as your child is older than 3 months, it may not make much of a difference what the thermometer reads. What actually matters is how your child is acting (or actually how your child is interacting, eating, and sleeping) and what other symptoms your child has (such as coughing or vomiting). The common questions in this chapter contain information and guidelines about fever and when you should call your pediatrician. I know I've said it before, but it's really true—as a parent, you know your child best, so if you feel something is wrong, never hesitate to call…anytime.

Who, What, When, Where, Why, and How?

> ## PEDIATRIC POINT
> ### Fever?
>
> Normal body temperature is around 98.6°F (37°C) and
> varies throughout the day. A temperature of 100.4°F
> (38°C) or higher, taken rectally, is considered a fever by
> most pediatricians.

49. What causes a fever? When do I need to call the doctor?

A fever is usually caused by infections from viruses (such as
a cold or the flu) or bacteria (such as strep throat or some
ear infections). Remember, the fever itself is not the disease,
only a sign that the body's defenses are trying to fight an
infection.

 No matter your child's age, some symptoms
along with fever warrant a more urgent call to
your pediatrician because they may indicate
a more serious illness or situation developing.
Call your doctor if your little one has a fever
and any of the following symptoms: refusal
or inability to drink fluids, seizure, continuous
crying, irritability after bringing down the fever
with appropriate medication, hard to wake up,
confusion, rash, stiff neck, trouble breathing,
persistent vomiting or diarrhea, or if the fever
persists for more than 3 days. If you think your
child really looks sick or you are worried about
something in particular, always call your doctor
regardless of your child's temperature.

The definition of fever for each age does vary slightly among pediatricians, but here are some general guidelines.

Newborn

Call immediately if your baby is *younger than 3 months* and has a temperature of *100.4°F (38°C) or higher.* If the pediatrician can't be reached, go to the emergency department.

Infant

If your infant is *older than 3 months* with a temperature above 102°F (39°C), call your pediatrician. The doctor will likely ask you about other symptoms (eg, cough, cold, vomiting, diarrhea) and how your child is acting overall to help determine if you need to bring your child in for evaluation or if you can wait and watch him at home for a few days.

Infant

Toddler

For children *older than 6 months,* a temperature of 104°F (40°C) or higher warrants a call (you'll probably be calling before you read this anyway). Otherwise, they can be watched at home as long as they are alert, interactive, and drinking fluids. If the symptoms aren't improving in 2 or 3 days or they are worsening, see your pediatrician.

50. How often do I need to take my child's temperature and what's the best way?

There is really no need to randomly check your child's temperature. If she feels unusually warm, is not eating well, or is acting irritable or overly sleepy, use a thermometer to check for a fever. For safety reasons, do not use a thermometer containing mercury because mercury spills from a broken thermometer can be dangerous.

Rectal temperatures are the most accurate and preferred method in newborns. Although the idea may seem uncomfortable to you, it won't hurt your baby. Just coat the end of the thermometer with a lubricant (such as water-based K-Y Jelly or petroleum-based Vaseline) and insert about half an inch (follow the instructions for your particular thermometer). Digital thermometers provide a quick, fairly accurate reading—within a minute you'll know your baby's temperature. If the thermometer reads 100.4°F (38°C) or higher, your newborn has a fever, which may sometimes indicate a serious infection. Although most newborn fevers are not serious, little ones can get very sick very quickly and should be evaluated as soon as possible— even if it means a trip to the emergency department in the middle of the night!

Immediately call your pediatrician if your newborn (any baby younger than 3 months) has a temperature of 100.4°F (38°C) or higher. If you have any concerns that your newborn might be sick—even in the absence of a fever—call your pediatrician.

Although rectal temperatures are most accurate, let's be practical. Your older infant or toddler is less likely to lie still long enough for you to get a good reading. For older infants and toddlers, a digital thermometer held under the arm, ear thermometer, or temporal artery thermometer is fine. If the thermometer reads 100.4°F (38°C) or higher, it's best to double-check rectally before calling your pediatrician, especially with an infant. No need to add or subtract a degree depending on where and how you take it. Just let your pediatrician know how the temperature was measured and how your child is acting.

PEDIATRIC POINT
Fever Feelings

All kids (and most adults too!) can feel and act miserable when they have a fever, no matter what other symptoms they have. What's important is how they are feeling when the fever comes down. If they are playing and running around the house, that's a good sign that they are probably not seriously ill.

 If your child is still not acting well once the fever comes down, call your pediatrician.

51. My child has a fever without any other symptoms. Do I need to take him to the doctor? When should I worry?

Newborn

If your baby is younger than 3 months and has a temperature of 100.4°F (38°C) or higher, always seek medical advice immediately and consult with your pediatrician. Newborns do not always show other signs of illness besides having a fever and they can get sick very quickly, so it's important not to wait.

Infant

Toddler

For older infants and toddlers, as long as they are acting well, you can observe them for a few days. With some viral infections, such as roseola (see Chapter 9, "Skin"), children can have a fever without any other symptoms for 2 or 3 days. The fever will go away and then there may be a rash (don't worry, it's not dangerous). With most other illnesses you will see some additional symptoms (eg, cough, runny nose, diarrhea) within 24 hours of the fever. Viral fevers can easily last for up to 4 or 5 days, but longer than that may mean there is another infection going on that may need treatment.

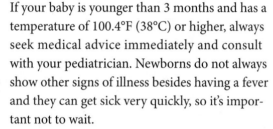

If your child has had a fever for more than 3 or 4 days without any other symptoms, call your pediatrician. The doctor will want to examine him and may possibly check his urine and even blood to make sure there isn't an infection hiding somewhere that hasn't yet presented itself.

52. My daughter has a fever. Do I need to give her medicine?

Newborn

Check with your pediatrician before giving your newborn any fever-reducing medication. And again, if your baby is younger than 3 months and has a fever, always call your doctor immediately or go to the emergency department.

Infant

Toddler

Remember that a fever is just a sign that your child's body is fighting an infection. The reason your doctor may recommend medicine to reduce a fever is so that your child may feel more comfortable (and therefore you will as well). When your child feels better, she will drink fluids (Popsicles work too) to help avoid dehydration that can occur with a fever. If she's acting well and drinking fluids, you don't have to give medicine because the fever itself isn't dangerous and will more than likely go away by itself.

Medication such as acetaminophen (Tylenol) or ibuprofen (Motrin or Advil) can be given in appropriate doses to reduce the fever. *Do not give your child aspirin* because it can cause Reye syndrome—a serious disease that can damage the brain and liver. Ibuprofen (only for infants older than 6 months) lasts 6 to 8 hours while acetaminophen lasts 4 to 6 hours. Both are dosed by weight, so be sure to check with your pediatrician or pharmacist if you are not sure of the correct dose for your child. To help avoid an accidental overdose, read package labels very carefully and always use the dropper or medicine cup that came with the specific medication you are giving.

Note: Infant's and children's formulations have different concentrations (see dosing charts on page 81). For example, 1 teaspoon (or 5 mL) of children's acetaminophen may be the proper dose for your 2-year-old, but the equivalent dose of infant's acetaminophen is only 2 full droppers (up to the top line) or 1.6 mL total. That's less than one third of the children's acetaminophen volume!

Call your pediatrician if your child is not acting well when the temperature comes down or if you find yourself needing to give these medications for more than 4 days.

Acetaminophen (Tylenol) Dosing Chart		
Child's Weight/ Approximate Age	**Infant's Concentrated Drops (80 mg/0.8 mL)**	**Children's Suspension Liquid (160 mg/5 mL) 5 mL = 1 tsp**
6–11 lb/ 0–5 mo	0.4 mL	
12–17 lb/ 6–11 mo	0.8 mL	½ tsp or 2.5 mL
18–23 lb/ 12–23 mo	1.2 mL (0.8 mL + 0.4 mL)	¾ tsp or 3.75 mL
24–35 lb/ 2–3 y	1.6 mL (0.8 mL + 0.8 mL)	1 tsp or 5 mL

Acetaminophen can be given every 4 to 6 hours as needed, up to 5 times a day.

Ibuprofen (Motrin or Advil) Dosing Chart		
Child's Weight/ Approximate Age	**Infant's Concentrated Drops (50 mg/1.25 mL)**	**Children's Suspension Liquid (100 mg/5 mL) 5 mL = 1 tsp**
6–11 lb/ 0–5 mo	Do not use.	Do not use.
12–17 lb/ 6–11 mo	1.25 mL	½ tsp or 2.5 mL
18–23 lb/ 12–23 mo	1.875 mL (1.25 mL + 0.625 mL)	¾ tsp or 3.75 mL
24–35 lb/ 2–3 y	2.50 mL (1.25 mL + 1.25 mL)	1 tsp or 5 mL

Ibuprofen can be given every 6 to 8 hours as needed, up to 4 times a day.

> ## DR. TANYA'S TIP
> ### Avoid Medication Mistakes
>
> - Read package labels very carefully.
> - Always use the dropper or medicine cup that comes with the specific medication you are giving.
> - Call your pediatrician if you are unsure about the appropriate dose for your child.
> - Keep a written log of the time and amount of medication given.
> - Do not give more than one medication at a time without consulting your physician.
> - Keep all medications safely out of your child's reach.
> - Make sure all caregivers are aware of the medication dose and when it needs to be given.

Other Fever Factors

53. Can teething cause a fever?

Although many parents sometimes notice that their child "feels warm" or "has a low-grade fever," teething does not actually cause a true fever. If your teething infant does have a fever, it is probably due to something else—possibly a cold or other illness that hasn't presented itself yet. Teething isn't always fun, even without a fever, as it can cause quite a bit of drool and fussiness as the teeth poke their way through sensitive gums—ouch! For infants (or even toddlers) who seem to be bothered by the situation, an appropriate dose of acetaminophen along with a cool teething ring to chew on (Popsicles work well for toddlers) may help. Depending on how high the temperature is and how your infant is acting, you can observe your teething child for a day or two or call your pediatrician for advice.

54. My child had his shots today. Now he has a fever. Should I worry?

Vaccines are important because they can protect your child from potentially dangerous and deadly diseases. Vaccines are safe and severe reactions are very rare. Mild reactions to vaccines such as a low-grade fever and fussiness may occur but fortunately do not last long. There may be some swelling, redness, and discomfort where the shot was given. Another common side effect from a shot is a small pea-sized lump under the skin at the site of injection. This is not dangerous and will resolve over the next few weeks.

Newborn

Although newborns may run a fever after receiving immunizations, check in with your pediatrician because any fever in a baby younger than 3 months should be evaluated.

Infant

Toddler

Some infants and toddlers will have a fever after their immunizations. Having a mild fever without any other symptoms is not dangerous. Give an appropriate dose of infant acetaminophen for a temperature above 100.4°F (38°C) or if your infant seems cranky. Your pediatrician may recommend a dose of acetaminophen just prior to the next set of vaccines or that you give acetaminophen as needed for the next 24 hours.

Remember, always call your pediatrician if your newborn's temperature is 100.4°F (38°C) or higher. For infants and toddlers, if fever persists for more than 24 hours or if the temperature is above 102°F (39°C), call your pediatrician.

Other very rare immunization side effects to call for include a rash all over the body, seizure, large amount of swelling around the shot or in the extremity used for the shot, persistent crying for more than 3 hours, or extreme lethargy.

55. Can a high temperature cause brain damage?

Developing brain damage from fevers is an urban legend. Fevers that are caused by infection do not cause brain damage. It takes an extremely high body temperature, such as 108°F (42.2°C), to cause brain damage. This can occur with high environmental temperatures such as those found in an enclosed car on a hot day, not typically from a common illness such as a cold or an ear infection. So the important lesson learned is to never leave your child alone in the car.

56. My child had a seizure. We took her to the emergency department. After examining her the doctor there told us it was a *febrile* seizure. What does this mean?

A febrile seizure is a type of seizure that occurs as a temperature is rising. Febrile seizures occur in fewer than 5% of children aged 6 months to 5 years. Children are more at risk when their body temperature rises extremely quickly. In fact, many parents don't even realize their child has a fever until they get to their pediatrician's office or the emergency department for evaluation of their child's seizure and the temperature is taken.

Although terrifying for parents to watch, febrile seizures are rarely dangerous and usually last for a few minutes. They will not cause brain damage and will not affect future intelligence or behavior. Having a febrile seizure does not necessarily mean that your child is going to develop a seizure disorder. About one third of all kids who have had a febrile seizure are at risk for having more, especially if there is a family history. If your child has had a febrile seizure, ask your pediatrician for more information. The doctor may recommend giving a fever reducer around the clock during times of illness.

 Although it may be stating the obvious, call your pediatrician the first time your child has a seizure so your child can be thoroughly evaluated. If your child has a known history of febrile seizures, discuss how to manage future fevers or seizures with your pediatrician, including the need to call if a seizure is different from previous episodes.

CHAPTER 8

Illnesses

"Daddy, I don't feel so good."

Many children spend a good portion of their toddlerhood continuously coughing with mucus running out of their nose. They seem to get better, return to preschool or attend a birthday party, and a few days later are home with something new. Luckily, with immunizations protecting our little ones from many potentially serious and life-threatening infections, most of what they easily pick up these days will also go away on its own (although it may first infect everyone else in your house).

It's never fun when one of your kids is sick (believe me, I know), especially since they always seem to be ill during an important work meeting or before a big family trip or event. So when can you wait? When should you call? And when do you need to seek medical attention right away? Here are the most common illness questions that parents and caregivers ask.

Suddenly Sick

57. How do I know if my baby is sick?

Newborn

Infant

Your baby can't tell you that he's not feeling well, but he will show you by changing his normal behavior. Sometimes the changes are subtle and sometimes more obvious, but changes from your baby's normal behavior and routine will be your tip-off that something may not be right. He may drink less, cry more, sleep more or less, breathe faster, have a fever, or just not look right to you. Babies are more susceptible to serious infections that can progress rapidly, so it is very important to call your doctor right away if you notice anything unusual. Trust your instincts. You know your baby's behaviors better than anyone else, so let your pediatrician know if something doesn't seem right.

Call your pediatrician immediately if your newborn has a temperature of 100.4°F (38°C) or higher (see Chapter 7, "Fever," for more information and instructions on how to take your baby's temperature). Other reasons to call your doctor include excessive fussiness, continuous crying, poor feeding, extreme sleepiness, rapid breathing, a decreased number of wet diapers, vomiting, sweating while feeding, or any blueness of the skin, especially around the mouth.

58. Why does it seem like my child is always sick? Could there be something wrong with her immune system?

Infant

Toddler

Healthy kids (with normal immune systems) can catch around 10 infections a year, especially if they are in child care or preschool. During the summer they tend to be mostly well, but it's common for them to bring home a new bug every 2 or 3 weeks during the winter. Most of the usual suspects (coughs and colds) are caused by viruses and will clear up on their own. Children pick up the colds from their friends or classmates—these bugs can survive on surfaces for hours and spread easily from person to person.

Often children are contagious before they become symptomatic. So even if no one appears to be sick, there still may be some sharing of germs that can cause illness. If your child seems to follow this pattern of frequent illnesses, although a nuisance, it is unlikely that anything is wrong with her immune system. Children who have problems with their immune system usually have recurrent unusual infections (not regular colds and coughs) such as serious pneumonias, skin abscesses, or meningitis (an infection around the brain and spinal cord) that often require hospitalization.

If your infant or toddler has been hospitalized several times with serious infections requiring antibiotics, talk to your pediatrician to see if any special testing is needed.

> ## DR. TANYA'S TIP
> ### Keeping Kids Germ Free
> Wash hands after playing, when entering the house, before eating, and after using the bathroom. Carry hand sanitizer (now available with lotion) or wipes in your bag for times when soap and water aren't available.

59. My child has a cold. Can I give him over-the-counter cold medicine?

Over-the-counter cough and cold medications aren't generally recommended for babies and toddlers. They have not been proven to help treat colds and there may be some unpleasant or potentially harmful side effects associated with them. Home remedies, herbal remedies, and supplements may also contain potentially dangerous ingredients, so always check with your pediatrician before giving anything to a young child.

If the cold is bothering your child, your best option is to try to clean out that stuffy nose so he can breathe and drink more easily. Place a drop or two of nasal saline in each nostril to loosen the mucus and help it drain. If the snot is interfering with sleep or feeding, try gentle suctioning. He won't like it, but if you can get the gunk out he'll feel better. A cool-mist humidifier or vaporizer at night may also help. For more tips on relieving nasal congestion and suctioning your little one's nose, refer to question #7, pages 11 through 13. As always, when your child is sick, make sure he drinks plenty of fluids.

Call your pediatrician or make an appointment for your child to be seen if the following is true:

Newborn

Your newborn has cold symptoms that are interfering with eating or sleeping, trouble breathing, or a fever.

Infant

Fevers persist for more than 3 to 4 days, cold symptoms last longer than 5 to 7 days without improvement, or breathing becomes very fast or seems labored.

Toddler

It's often OK if cold symptoms (such as cough and runny nose) linger for more than a week in this age group. Call if symptoms seem to be worsening after 5 to 7 days or are keeping him up at night. In addition, your toddler should be evaluated for any fever persisting more than 4 days or if a new fever appears after several days of having a cold.

Eyes and Ears and Mouth and Nose

60. My child woke up with red eyes and green eye discharge. Is this pinkeye? Does she need eyedrops? When can she return to preschool?

Infant

Toddler

Pinkeye (conjunctivitis) is like a cold, but in the eye. It is very contagious and easily spreads from child to child since they often touch their eyes with contaminated hands. It can be caused by a virus, which will get better on its own, or a bacteria that needs treatment with antibiotic eye medication. A good rule of thumb is that antibiotic eye medication may be needed if there is yellow or green discharge, especially if the eyelids are stuck shut on waking. If the eyes are just red without any discharge or with clear discharge, you may be able to wait. It should clear up on its own within a few days. If your child also has a cold or fever, is uncomfortable, or isn't acting well, see your pediatrician because an ear or a sinus infection can sometimes accompany the eye infection. Your child can usually return to child care or school 24 hours after eye medication has been started or when the discharge is gone.

 Call your pediatrician about your child's symptoms to see if your child needs an appointment or a prescription.

61. My baby has a cold and is tugging on his ears. Could he have an ear infection? Does he need an antibiotic?

In general, ear tugging is not a reliable indicator of an ear infection. However, if your baby has had a cold for several days and now has a fever, is fussy, is waking up at night, or is eating and drinking less, it's a good idea to have his ears checked. Even if he has had an ear infection before or was in yesterday for a cold, the ears need to be checked again. Ears can become infected overnight, so an ear examination can really change in one day. Examining the ears is important because it helps doctors determine if an antibiotic is needed and if so, which antibiotic to use. Not all ear infections need an antibiotic. Some are viral and will go away on their own. Depending on your child's age, other symptoms (eg, fever, pain), and how the ear looks on examination, your pediatrician will decide whether an antibiotic is needed or if a wait-and-see approach can be taken. With the wait-and-see approach, you may be instructed to call or start treatment if fever, pain, or other symptoms appear or current symptoms worsen. Your pediatrician may advise you to bring your child back for an ear recheck a few days later or after any treatment is complete to see if the infection is truly gone and if there is any remaining fluid.

It is true that some children are just more prone to ear infections than others. But certain factors can increase your child's risk such as sleeping with a bottle, attending child care, and exposure to secondhand smoke. How can you *decrease* your child's risk? If possible, avoid these risk factors. Also, breastfed infants get fewer ear infections—one more reason to breastfeed your little one!

62. My child is prone to ear infections. Does she need ear tubes?

Possibly. Ear tubes (pressure equalization tubes, sometimes called myringotomy or tympanostomy tubes) get rid of or at least significantly reduce ear infections—it's amazing how they can change your child's (and your) life. Your pediatrician may recommend that your child see a specialist for ear tubes if she has had the following:

- Three to 4 ear infections in 6 months or 4 to 6 infections in 12 months
- Three back-to-back antibiotics for an ear infection
- Three months of persistent fluid behind the eardrum
- Hearing loss or speech delay

During this very simple and common surgery, small tubes (like tiny straws) are placed in the eardrums to allow air to get behind the eardrum and fluid to drain as needed. They typically fall out with time and the eardrum heals on its own.

PEDIATRIC POINT
Middle Versus Outer Ear Infection

Middle Ear Infection: Otitis Media
This occurs when fluid becomes infected behind the eardrum. This type of infection is more likely when your child has a cold.

Outer Ear Infection: Otitis Externa (Swimmer's Ear)
This occurs when the skin lining the ear canal becomes infected. It is usually caused by water getting trapped or trauma (such as from a cotton swab); bacteria then grows. Outer ear infections are very painful, especially when you touch or tug on the ear. Treatment is with antibiotic eardrops.

63. My child has a fever and is refusing to drink. I think his throat or mouth is hurting. What could it be?

There are many infections that can cause your little one's mouth or throat to hurt. For children younger than 3 years, most infections are viral and will improve on their own in about a week. The most important thing is to keep him well hydrated, so let him drink anything that he likes. Some children need a little encouragement, but most can be coaxed to take small sips with a straw. Popsicles work well too! Your pediatrician may also recommend acetaminophen or ibuprofen for the pain.

Here's a rundown on the most common sore throat or mouth illnesses.

- **Hand, foot, and mouth disease:** In addition to fever for a few days with painful sores in the mouth, there is often a blister-like rash on the hands, feet, and sometimes the diaper area. The rash may also be tender, especially on the bottom of the feet, so your child may not want to walk. Fortunately, the discomfort will soon pass and nothing needs to be applied to the rash. All symptoms are caused by a coxsackievirus and will improve on their own. Your pediatrician may advise you to try acetaminophen or ibuprofen for the discomfort.
- **Sore throat and pink eyes:** Again, just a virus, usually adenovirus to be exact. The back of the throat can look very red and may even have pus on it. It is not strep throat (which is caused by a bacteria) and does not need antibiotics. The virus also causes the white part of the

eyes to look pink, sometimes with a sticky discharge. This pink eye needs no treatment and will get better on its own.

- **Major mouth ulcers:** Although several viruses can cause a few white ulcers (sores) in the mouth or throat, if your child's mouth and tongue are covered with them and he is in lots of pain he may have a common childhood herpes virus infection. In some cases an antiviral medication or strong pain reliever may be prescribed. It is very important that you encourage your child to drink. Despite everyone's best efforts, some children are in so much discomfort that they will completely refuse to drink. In such cases, hospitalization for intravenous fluids may be necessary.

- **Strep throat:** Usually not very common in this age group unless a close family member has it, strep throat symptoms are a fever and sore throat *without* cold symptoms (runny nose and cough). In this age group there may also be stomach pain, headache, vomiting, or a rash. Strep throat with a rash is called scarlet fever. Sounds scary, but it is treated with the same antibiotics as regular strep throat. Reassure grandparents that because we now have antibiotics to treat the infection, scarlet fever is no longer as dangerous as it was years ago!

Newborn

As always, call or see your pediatrician if your newborn has a fever, is drinking less, refuses 2 or more feedings in a row, or looks sick.

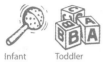

Infant   Toddler

Call or see your pediatrician if the fever lasts more than 3 days, your child isn't drinking well, or he looks really sick.

64. My child has green nasal discharge. Does she need an antibiotic?

Despite what your mother may have told you, green does not always mean antibiotics are needed. Plenty of viruses (common colds) cause green mucus that goes away on its own. If your child has a clear runny nose for more than a week or two and then it turns green or she gets a fever or seems like she is in pain (eg, fussy, irritable), she should be examined because she may have developed a sinus or an ear infection. Please don't ask for an antibiotic to be prescribed over the phone. Your child should always be examined first to know exactly what is going on and what needs to be treated.

Coughing and Wheezing

65. My child wheezes and coughs when he gets a cold. Does this mean he has asthma?

Possibly. Colds (also called upper respiratory tract infections) are the most common cause of wheezing in infants and toddlers. Their small airways easily get inflamed and narrow when triggered by an infection. Most physicians will call it asthma after a few such episodes or if the wheezing recurs over a period of several months or years. No matter what it is called, if your child is truly wheezing, asthma medications may be needed to help your child breathe more easily and prevent future episodes of wheezing. A bronchodilator (such as albuterol or levalbuterol) is often given via

nebulizer or inhaler to help open the airways and make it
easier for your child to breathe during an episode. Oral ste-
roids may be needed for a few days to decrease the inflammation and mucus in your child's lungs. In addition, your
child may be placed on a daily medication (inhaled or oral)
to protect the airways and prevent wheezing year-round
or at least during the winter months when colds are more
prevalent. As your child grows, the airways grow and this
problem may go away. If you have a family history of
asthma, allergies, or eczema, there is a chance that your
child's symptoms will persist and he will officially be
diagnosed with asthma.

Let your pediatrician know if you think your
child may be wheezing. The doctor will listen to
your child's lungs and prescribe appropriate
treatment.

66. What is RSV? Is my child at risk?

RSV stands for respiratory syncytial virus. In older children
and adults it causes a cold with a really runny, goopy nose—
the one you get almost every winter. In young children, the
infection can range from minor cold symptoms to serious
lung problems, usually depending on their age and previous
medical history (such as premature birth, heart disease, or
lung disease). RSV is most common during the winter.

Newborn

Infant

In newborns and infants, RSV can migrate into
the lungs and cause bronchiolitis, an inflammation and infection of the tiny airways of the
lungs. It can cause very serious trouble breathing
and wheezing, especially in babies who were
born prematurely or who have heart or lung

disease. For these high-risk babies there is a shot available called palivizumab (Synagis) to help protect them from catching RSV. It is given once a month from October through April, when RSV is most prevalent. Ask your pediatrician if your infant qualifies. There is no medication to treat RSV, only symptomatic care such as suctioning the nasal congestion. Even asthma medications that are often used to treat wheezing caused by asthma rarely will help wheezing from RSV. If your infant is having trouble breathing, she may need to be hospitalized for oxygen, breathing treatments, or fluids.

Call your pediatrician right away if your infant has a cold and is breathing fast (more than 60 times a minute), you hear wheezing, you notice retractions (skin sucking in above or below the ribs with each breath), or she is having trouble eating, drinking, or sleeping.

Toddler

Most toddlers with RSV have a runny, goopy nose. Some may develop bronchiolitis (as discussed for newborns and infants on the previous page) but can usually be cared for at home after an examination by your pediatrician. Because RSV is a virus, as long as there is not any associated trouble breathing, the illness will improve on its own. RSV is extremely contagious so it is a good idea to keep your toddler away from newborns and help her frequently wash her hands.

If your toddler has any wheezing or trouble breathing, call your pediatrician.

PEDIATRIC POINT
Influenza (the Actual Flu)

When many parents hear the word flu they immediately think of vomiting and diarrhea. The actual flu is a respiratory illness, not a stomach bug. Symptoms include high fever (temperature usually above 102°F [39°C]), body aches, sore throat, runny nose, cough, and extreme fatigue. For an otherwise healthy person, having the flu is probably the worst you will ever feel. Symptoms last for about a week, but some children get much sicker and need to be hospitalized. Unfortunately, the flu still causes thousands of deaths each year.

The best way to protect your family from the flu is to vaccinate. The flu vaccine is recommended yearly for everyone 6 months and older. It can be given as a shot or as a nasal spray, which is currently approved for children older than 2 years. And no, you can't catch the flu from the vaccine.

If you think anyone in your family has the flu, see your physician as soon as possible. In some cases your doctor may prescribe an antiviral medication to help reduce the severity of flu symptoms and decrease the chance that the rest of your family catches the virus.

67. My child has a bad cough. Should I bring him in? How do I know if he has pneumonia?

Many coughs are caused by postnasal drip from a cold rather than an actual lung infection such as pneumonia. So how do you know the difference? In general, if your child has a runny nose and is acting well between bouts of coughing, you may be able to just keep an eye on him at home. Although a cough can sometimes linger for a few weeks, it shouldn't be getting any worse after 4 or 5 days. If your child starts to have fast breathing, the cough isn't beginning to improve after a week or is worsening, or a fever appears, be sure to have your doctor examine your child because sometimes serious infections such as pneumonia can develop. In such cases, antibiotics may be needed to treat the infection.

 Call your doctor right away if there are any signs of trouble breathing such as wheezing, skin sucking in above or below the ribs (retractions), stomach moving in and out with each breath, or chest pain. In addition, if the cough is keeping him up all night or he has a high fever, call for an appointment.

68. My child woke up last night with a horrible, barking cough—like a seal. What is it?

In general, seal bark = croup. Croup is a viral infection that causes swelling of the upper airway, voice box, and windpipe (not the lungs). It produces a distinctive barky, seal-like cough and hoarse voice. Older kids and adults usually only get a loud cough and hoarse voice or just cold symptoms. Because it's a virus, antibiotics won't help.

In newborns, infants, and toddlers, the inflammation can sometimes be severe enough to produce stridor—a loud, harsh sound heard when your child breathes in that may be associated with trouble breathing. The second or third night tends to be worse, so even if your child seems fine the next day, talk to your pediatrician to see if treatment is needed.

To help decrease stridor, spend 20 minutes with your child outside in the cool night air or in a steam-filled bathroom. Running a humidifier or vaporizer in her bedroom at night may also help.

 If the stridor isn't improving or worsens, your child is having trouble breathing, or your child can't swallow well or is drooling, call your pediatrician, go to the emergency department, or call 911. Your child may need a steroid medication or special inhaled treatment to decrease the inflammation and make it easier to breathe.

PEDIATRIC POINT
Nighttime Cough Keeping You Up?

A nighttime cough without fever or other symptoms may not be an infection. Cough, especially at night, is a common hallmark of asthma. Coughing can also indicate drainage from the nose or sinuses into the throat while lying down, which could be caused by allergies or an infection (cold or sinus). A thorough history and examination by your pediatrician can usually determine the cause of the cough and treatment can be provided as needed.

Returning to Activities

69. My son is getting over a cold. When can he return to child care or preschool, or attend a birthday party or other event?

Generally speaking, he can be around other kids once his fever has been gone for 24 hours and he's feeling better. If your child has been placed on an antibiotic for any reason, he should receive the medication for at least 24 hours before being around other children. If he's vomiting, having massive diarrhea, or coughing up a storm, obviously he should rest at home and not be around other kids until these symptoms are more under control. Often it's the milder symptoms (such as slight runny nose and cough) that leave parents wondering what to do. Only you can make that game-day decision, but be considerate of others—before you take him out, think to yourself, would I want another child with the same symptoms around my son? You can always check with your child care or preschool; they may have specific guidelines for when previously sick children can return.

Vaccines

70. Vaccine information is everywhere and it seems so overwhelming. What do I need to know?

Thanks to vaccines, many diseases that once caused death and disability in children are now rare in the United States. But although they may be rare, they aren't gone. Many of these infections are only a plane ride away, just waiting to make a huge comeback—which will happen if people stop vaccinating. I have seen children get seriously ill, become permanently disabled, and even die from vaccine-preventable diseases such as meningitis, chickenpox, and whooping cough. By vaccinating, you not only protect your own child, but also help to shield others who are at increased risk such as newborns, friends receiving chemotherapy, and elderly grandparents.

Vaccines are very safe but may have minor side effects. Your child may experience soreness at the injection site, have a mild fever, be slightly cranky, or even sleep a little longer than usual (enjoy this one) the day or two after some vaccines are given. Your pediatrician may recommend giving an appropriate dose of acetaminophen or, if your baby is older than 6 months, ibuprofen prior to the vaccines and as needed later that day. Another common side effect from any shot is a small pea-sized lump under the skin at the injection site. This is not dangerous and will resolve over the next few weeks.

Risk of a serious side effect from a vaccine is very small compared with the risk of serious illness caused by catching the disease. There are countless medical studies that support the safety of vaccines and show that vaccines do not cause autism or any other childhood disease. Much parental concern has been focused on thimerosal, a mercury-based preservative. It is important to know that thimerosal was removed from all childhood vaccines by 2001 as a precautionary measure. Therefore, none of the vaccines that your little one will get contain this preservative.

Call your pediatrician if your child experiences any of the following symptoms after receiving vaccines: fever for more than 24 hours or temperature above 103°F (39.4°C), inconsolable crying for more than 3 hours, extreme lethargy, rash all over the body, seizure, or large amount of swelling around the shot or in the extremity used for the shot.

For more information on vaccines, speak with your pediatrician and visit the American Academy of Pediatrics and Centers for Disease Control and Prevention Web sites (www.aap.org and www.cdc.gov, respectively).

CHAPTER 9

Skin

"The skinny on skin"

After soaking in amniotic fluid for 9 months (kind of like an extended spa vacation), you'd expect your newborn to have silky, soft, clear skin. While some do, more often than not, babies have dry, cracked skin that may be followed by an assortment of bumps and blemishes throughout the first year or so of life. Although many of these rashes resolve on their own, other skin conditions can pop up during the first few years. Some are a result of dry weather or irritating soaps. Many come hand-in-hand with a variety of viral illnesses picked up from playmates or siblings. And some rashes occur for no apparent reason at all.

Even though the red blotches may not bother the affected child, rashes in general can be bothersome for parents and caregivers. The following questions and answers help demystify some of the more common red or dry patches you may discover under your child's clothes. However, when it comes to a rash, often a picture is worth a thousand words. So don't be surprised if you need to break out your camera or take a trip to your pediatrician's office to get to the bottom of the blotch.

Jaundice

71. My newborn is yellow. My mother says it is "jaundice." What does that mean? Should I be worried?

Newborn

Your mom is right. The yellowish color of the skin is called *jaundice*—a common occurrence in newborns. The first hint of yellow typically appears on the face and then progresses down the body. In otherwise healthy infants, it is usually at its worst around day 4 or 5 of life and then begins to resolve, although the yellow color on the face and in the whites of the eyes can linger for a week or two.

It may reassure you to know that most babies turn a bit yellow after birth; some are just more noticeable than others. It develops from a very normal process that occurs in all babies by the breakdown of red blood cells. The normal breakdown of red blood cells produces bilirubin. This occurs in the liver and is excreted in the intestines (in the form of poop!). Because this excretion process is very immature, some babies just can't keep up and extra bilirubin lingers in the blood and then gets deposited in the skin, causing the yellow color.

While some degree of jaundice is very normal in newborns, it can sometimes indicate a more serious problem. That is why it is important to let your pediatrician know if your baby begins to look yellow. In addition to a quick history and physical examination, a simple blood or skin test may be needed to help determine your baby's bilirubin level and allow your pediatrician to advise on any necessary treatment.

The most common reason for jaundice is breastfeeding jaundice. This usually occurs in the first week when the baby is not taking in enough milk, either because mom's milk supply is not fully in or the baby has yet to master the art of nursing. Your pediatrician may advise you to increase your breastfeeding or even give supplemental formula to make sure your baby receives enough liquid to poop adequately and clear the bilirubin.

Take-home message: The more your baby eats and poops, the more bilirubin will be cleared from the body, and the sooner the jaundice will resolve.

 Let your pediatrician know if your baby starts to look yellow so the doctor can assess the situation and check a bilirubin level if needed. In some instances, newborns with high bilirubin levels may benefit from extra fluids or require treatment with special lights.

Infant

Toddler

Jaundice that develops outside of the immediate newborn period (after the first few weeks) is not normal and should be evaluated by your pediatrician ASAP because it could be the sign of an infection or liver disease. If you think your infant or toddler's skin has a yellow or orange hue, but the whites of her eyes are still white, you can relax as chances are that the skin is discolored from eating too many carotene-containing foods such as carrots, sweet potatoes, and squash. In this case, you may notice that your child's palms, soles, and face (especially the tip of her nose) are a little more yellow than the rest of her body. No need to intervene, except maybe to back off a little on yellow and orange veggies in favor of green ones.

If your infant or toddler has true jaundice (skin as well as the whites of the eyes are yellow), call your pediatrician.

Rashes

72. What are the best creams for diaper rash?

The diaper cream you choose will depend on the type of diaper rash your baby has. In the first week of life, diaper rashes are often simply due to irritation from wetness. Applying a barrier cream that contains zinc oxide (such as Desitin or Balmex) is generally best for creating a barrier between a baby's sensitive skin and irritants, but even a thin layer of petroleum jelly (as found in Vaseline, Aquaphor, or A&D ointment) can work well in preventing many common newborn rashes (not to mention help in making stool easier to wipe off!). If, however, your baby has a rash that is bright reddish pink and raised or sometimes raw, often with little bumps surrounding it, chances are you're looking at a yeast infection. In such cases, you will need a special yeast cream (see question #73 on the next page). Whenever your baby's diaper rash doesn't improve after a few days with the cream of your choice, or if you have questions about how to best treat it in the first place, be sure to have your pediatrician check it out.

DR. TANYA'S TIP
Sensitive Baby Bottoms

In the newborn nursery, damp gauze pads may have been used to clean your baby's bottom, leaving many parents to wonder what they should use when they get home. Although alcohol-free, unscented diaper wipes are fine, I prefer using something even a little gentler during the first 2 weeks or so. Dipping a very soft paper towel or a soft baby washcloth (if you're OK washing them afterward) in warm water works well for sensitive bottoms. After the first few weeks, go ahead and buy unscented, alcohol-free diaper wipes by the case, but if your little one (or even your toddler) is prone to getting really impressive diaper rashes, switching back to soft cloths or paper towels can help.

73. Why do babies get rashes from yeast and how do I clear it up?

Yeast grows best in warm, moist places…like your baby's diaper area! The typical yeast rash is hot pinkish-red, raised, and quite "angry" looking. It often has several small spots that extend beyond the main area of the rash. A yeast rash is caused by an infection of the skin by a type of yeast called *Candida albicans.* While this yeast is very common in babies and causes its fair share of distress (for babies and their parents), it is fortunately not truly dangerous. Getting rid of a yeast infection requires a special cream to clear it up. I find that using a prescription ointment containing a combination of 3 ingredients—an antifungal medication to clear up the yeast along with zinc oxide and petroleum jelly to protect the skin and help it heal—works especially well. Alternatively, your pediatrician may advise you to layer an over-the-counter yeast cream with a zinc oxide diaper cream on top with every diaper change. While you are waiting for the rash to go away, soaking in an oatmeal bath can help soothe your baby's sore bottom.

74. I thought my baby would have soft, beautiful, clear skin, yet it seems like there's always a bump or blemish somewhere. Why is this and what can I do?

Newborn

There are an assortment of newborn rashes; although they are not serious and do resolve over time, they can throw a wrench into your plans for a baby announcement photo shoot. Here are the most common.

Erythema toxicum (also called E tox): This common newborn rash typically develops on the second or third day of life. It tends to look quite a bit like bug bites—the skin has several white, blister-like bumps with an area of redness surrounding each blister. E tox can occur anywhere on the body. No one knows exactly what causes this, but there's no need to be concerned. Once your pediatrician confirms the diagnosis, you can rest assured that this newborn rash is harmless and usually resolves on its own by 2 to 4 weeks of age. In the meantime, leave the blisters alone.

Baby acne: Yes, babies can get acne too! This undesirable, yet relatively harmless baby rash usually shows up at 3 or 4 weeks after birth and for many babies, improves by 2 or 3 months. Exposure to the hormones that are transferred from mom to baby are often to blame. Most of the time, the best treatment for baby acne is no treatment at all. You can simply continue to gently wash your baby's skin with plain water or a mild fragrance-free baby soap or shampoo. In addition, ask your pediatrician if it might help to use 1% hydrocortisone on specific spots once or twice a day for 1 or 2 days to temporarily tame them for a special event or photo. Don't worry, just because your infant develops acne does not mean he will have more acne as a teen.

Cradle cap (seborrheic dermatitis): Cradle cap is basically the baby equivalent of dandruff. These dry, flaky patches commonly occur on the scalp and eyebrows. In its mild form, treatment typically involves daily shampooing combined with gentle brushing of the scales using a baby brush or soft washcloth. There are several infant cradle cap shampoos on the market that you may wish to try. For more pronounced cases, your pediatrician may recommend an adult dandruff shampoo or antifungal shampoo be applied to your baby's scalp like lotion, massaged in, and then rinsed off. It is important to be careful not to get these products in a baby's eyes. While petroleum jelly products and vegetable oil may also work well to clear up cradle cap, if your child has a full head of hair, they can be somewhat greasy and challenging to wash out. Sometimes 1% hydrocortisone cream can also be used, especially when treating eyebrows. If your baby's cradle cap is leaving you scratching your head, be sure to go over a plan of action with your pediatrician at your next well-baby examination.

75. My daughter came home from child care with a rash all over. She's acting normal. Do I need to bring her to the office?

Infant

Toddler

My general rule of thumb is that if it isn't bothering her, it doesn't bother me. However, since it will bother most child care providers, a trip to the pediatrician is often needed for evaluation and a note stating when it is safe to return to child care or preschool. Many things including an infection (such as a virus) or contact with an irritating substance (such as soap or drool) can cause a rash, often without other symptoms. If this is the case, it's OK to keep an eye on the rash for a few days.

 If the rash worsens or isn't improving within 2 or 3 days, it begins bothering her, or she starts acting sick, call your pediatrician.

76. My child had a fever for 3 days without any other symptoms. The fever went away, but now he has a rash. What should I do?

Infant

Toddler

While it's always a good idea to touch base with your pediatrician, in most instances like this, parents don't need to do anything at all as long as their child is feeling all right. These symptoms are quite suggestive of a classic childhood viral infection known as roseola. Fever (temperature often 102°F [39°C] or higher) without any other symptoms can leave parents and pediatricians alike looking for answers. After about 3 days, the answer usually becomes quite clear as the fever resolves and is followed within a day or so by a telltale roseola rash. By the time the rash appears, children are no longer contagious and can return—rash and all—to normal activities (eg, preschool, mommy-and-me class).

77. After a week of a stuffy, runny nose, my child has little honey-colored crusty scabs on her face. What is this and how do I clear it up?

Infant

Toddler

It sounds like your child may have impetigo—an infection of the skin that is caused by one of two types of common bacteria (staph and strep) that dwell in many people's noses and on their skin. Classically, these honey-crusted sores are found on the face, often appearing during or after a cold or sinus infection. The excess nasal drainage (not to mention little fingers poking around) increases the likelihood that these nose-dwelling bacteria will spread to surrounding skin. You'll want to see your pediatrician to confirm the diagnosis and get proper treatment. Topical antibiotic ointment is often used to clear up impetigo, but if there are many lesions, it is spreading, or it keeps recurring despite the use of an ointment, oral antibiotics may be needed to get rid of the infection.

78. My son has a tender, red, raised area on his leg. I'm not sure what happened, but I think it's infected. What do I do?

Toddler

Any break in the skin—whether from a cut, scrape or insect bite—has the potential to get infected. Whenever an area of skin becomes tender or red or contains pus, it is important to seek medical attention right away because bacterial infections of the skin are serious business and can spread quickly if not evaluated and treated appropriately.

Methicillin-resistant *Staphylococcus aureus* (MRSA) is a bad bug (technically a bacteria, but often referred to as a bug, nonetheless). Like other types of staph, MRSA can live on your skin or in your nose unnoticed until a simple scrape or scratch allows it to get through the skin's defenses and boom—you may be faced with a bad skin infection. Infections often start out looking like a pimple or a bite and may progress rather quickly. In addition, the affecting bacteria can stick around in your house and wreak havoc on all who enter. In the case of MRSA, the resulting skin infection is particularly difficult to treat because this type of staph is resistant to many common antibiotics used for skin infections. Close medical supervision and specific antibiotics are needed to treat MRSA. Sometimes drainage of the infected pus is needed. To prevent infection of other family members and to get rid of any lingering bacteria from your home, your doctor may recommend some of the following:

- Use an antibiotic ointment (mupirocin) in all household noses twice a day for about a week.
- Add bleach (one teaspoon of regular strength bleach per gallon of water) to the bath and soak for 15 minutes twice a week. Just be sure to air out the bathroom well, especially if your child has asthma.
- Clean skin with an over-the-counter anti-microbial soap (such as Hibiclens).

- Wash towels daily in hot water and dry on a high heat setting.
- Keep fingernails clean and short to prevent scratching and spreading.

 With any skin infection, a fever can mean the bacteria has spread into the bloodstream, so call your doctor immediately. Hospitalization with intravenous antibiotics may be needed.

PEDIATRIC POINT
Slather the Sunscreen

Children have very sensitive skin and can burn easily if exposed to the sun. Even little ones with darker skin are at risk. To protect your child from an uncomfortable sunburn and skin cancer later in life, keep your child's skin covered with light clothing and keep her out of direct sunlight as much as possible. You can also purchase clothing with built-in sun protection.

For babies younger than 6 months, sunscreen may be used on small areas of the body such as the face and back of the hands if adequate clothing and shade are not available. After 6 months of age, slather her with sunscreen (look for broad-spectrum and SPF 30 or higher) 30 minutes prior to heading outdoors. Barrier sunscreens such as zinc oxide or titanium dioxide are usually best. Whichever brand you choose, test it out on your baby's back for a reaction before applying it all over. Reapply frequently—every 1 to 2 hours and after getting wet or sweating. Sunglasses with UV protections will shield her eyes and a hat will protect her head. Keeping them on is challenging, but play a game or make a fun name for it (robot glasses or zookeeper hat) and be a good role model with sun protection yourself.

Things That Make You Itch

79. What is eczema and how do I treat it?

Eczema, or atopic dermatitis, is a chronic, allergic skin condition. It is most common in infants and young children with a family history of asthma and allergies. Patchy areas of skin become dry, itchy, and irritated. In more serious cases, there may also be redness, swelling, cracking, weeping, crusting, or scaling. Eczema can be triggered by any number of factors, including food, soap, detergent, temperature changes, sweating, or other things that irritate or dry out the skin. For some children, flare-ups are few and far between. Others may be faced with ongoing symptoms that can vary considerably in severity, ranging from mild to quite widespread.

While eczema itself is a condition that can't technically be cured, children often outgrow it. In the meantime, it is entirely possible to treat eczema and prevent its symptoms from recurring. First, stay away from anything that you know causes the rash in your child. Often though, it isn't one specific thing, but a combination of things that can trigger the eczema. Decreasing all allergenic or drying substances in your child's environment can help and is not as daunting as it may seem. For example, use laundry detergent that is free of perfume and dye. At the same time, steer clear of fabric softeners; they are not recommended for children with eczema. Similarly, soap should be mild and unscented. Remember that water, especially if it is soapy, can dry the skin. Instead of rubbing your child's skin dry after a short bath, gently pat it and slather a mild, unscented ointment or thick cream all over. It's best to get the ointment or cream on within 3 minutes of getting out of the bath

before the water evaporates and dries the skin even more.
Use ointment or cream twice a day on your little one to keep
skin hydrated and to better prevent bad, uncomfortable
flare-ups. When your child's eczema worsens, talk to your
pediatrician, as there are many steroid and nonsteroid
creams that can be used on a regular or an as-needed basis.
If your child is up all night itching and scratching (which
can increase infection as well as delay healing), your pediatrician may recommend an antihistamine.

 If you see any oozing, pus, or increasing redness
and tenderness of the skin, or if your child develops a fever, call your pediatrician—these can all
be signs of a skin infection.

80. Yikes! My daughter broke out in an itchy, welt-like rash (hives) while we were eating at a restaurant. What should I do?

Whenever a child seems to be reacting to something she
ate or came into contact with, be sure that the rash is not
accompanied by any more concerning signs of an allergic
reaction such as wheezing, trouble swallowing, or facial
swelling. Once you've determined that you're only dealing
with an itchy rash with areas of raised red bumps, sometimes with pale centers, it is quite likely that she has hives.
Hives may appear all over the body almost instantly (or
within a few hours) after eating or touching something
specific. Or hives may occur on one area of the body,
disappear, and reappear later somewhere else. Foods (such
as milk, eggs, nuts, and shellfish), medication (such as peni-
cillin), or a bee sting can all cause hives. In addition, hives

can accompany a number of viral infections. Although frequently the cause cannot be identified, make a list of everything that your child ate (such as food or medication) or touched several hours before the rash appeared, as well as any recent bee stings or illnesses. Take the list to your pediatrician to help identify any potential cause for the hives, and often more pressing at the moment, discuss how to take the itch out of the situation. Your pediatrician may recommend giving an oral antihistamine (like Benadryl) to offer some relief. In cases in which hives keep showing up or are particularly itchy, you may want to get additional advice about using a non-sedating antihistamine around the clock for a few days because the use of regular antihistamines can make children quite drowsy. If you have an allergic infant or child, it is wise to be prepared and have an antihistamine on hand at all times, just in case.

 Allergic reactions that cause trouble breathing can quickly become life threatening. If your child starts wheezing, has trouble swallowing, or develops any swelling of the face, tongue, throat, or neck, it is important to seek medical care immediately at the emergency department or by calling 911. Talk to your pediatrician about whether a referral to an allergist is needed to determine what caused the reaction and assess your child's risk.

81. Ughhh! We seem to have head lice. How do I get rid of it?

No doubt about it, those pesky little critters can be a pain for parents and children. Unfortunately, they can spread relatively easily from one child to the next because lice can crawl (but not fly or jump) from head to head and are commonly transferred by simply sharing hats and brushes. That said, most cases of head lice can be treated relatively easily. Try over-the-counter lice shampoo applied to a dry scalp and hair and leave on for as long as recommended. Finally, comb out every nit (the tiny whitish-gray eggs) from your child's head—this can be very time consuming if there is a lot of hair! If you're not having much luck eliminating the lice, there is also a prescription-strength shampoo available, so call your pediatrician.

PEDIATRIC POINT
Got Pinworms?

Pinworms, although not fun to find, are essentially harmless. They look like little whitish-grey threads, popping up on a child's bottom (on the skin around the anus, to be exact) usually at night. Symptoms include nighttime itching of the bottom or even the vaginal area in girls. Treatment consists of a one-time chewable prescription tablet, often repeated in 2 weeks. Your pediatrician may also advise treating other family members. Wash all clothes and bedding in hot water to reduce the risk of reinfection.

Birthmarks

82. My baby has a birthmark. What is it and will it go away?

Some will disappear, some will fade, and some will stay. Here are the most common birthmarks.

Stork bite or angel kiss (nevus simplex): Remember when your mom and dad told you that the stork brought new babies into the world? The term stork bite comes from this fable and looks like a flat, pink or red mark on the back of the neck. The same type of birthmark on the forehead or eyelids is often called an angel kiss. These harmless birthmarks may become more noticeable when a baby cries or during a bath because of an increase in body temperature and blood flow. Their presence is often short-lived, as most fade with time and are hardly noticeable by 4 or 5 years of age.

Hemangioma: This type of birthmark is also red, but often looks more like a bloodred, raised, strawberry-type lesion. Made up of a cluster of tiny blood vessels, hemangiomas often become bigger and more pronounced before getting better. That's because hemangiomas typically grow in size over the first year of life and then begin to shrink and fade from the center out. By the age of 5 years, about 50% will have disappeared. By the age of 10, 90% will be gone. These birthmarks do not need to be treated or removed unless they are located in areas where they may interfere with important functions such as over the eyes (where they may interfere with vision) or in the mouth or throat (where they can interfere with breathing or eating). Other reasons to remove this type of birthmark are cosmetic (some specialists recommend surgically removing any large hemangioma on the face) or those in locations easily bumped, since hemangiomas are prone to bleeding.

Mongolian spot: Often confused with a bruise early on, this birthmark looks bluish-gray and is most commonly located on the back or buttocks. Mongolian spots are more common in darker skinned babies, tend to fade by school age, and are not dangerous.

CHAPTER 10

Ingestions, Injuries, and First Aid

"Owies and other bumps in the road"

Sometimes injuries happen. It would be nice if we could protect our children from danger 100% of the time, but that's just not realistic. To add insult to the injury, kids climb and jump when we'd like them to sit still, and they touch and eat things that we thought were out of their reach. Fortunately, most of the time it isn't serious, but some injuries can be life threatening. Do your best to protect your children—always buckle them up in properly installed car seats, baby proof your house, and keep a close eye on your little ones when you are out. Even with the most vigilant care and best baby-proofing skills, injuries may still happen, so it is just as important for you to be prepared and know what to do should the need arise.

DR. TANYA'S TIP

Emergency Information

Keep the following on your refrigerator, near a house phone, and in your cell phone or PDA:

- Child's name, birth date, and current weight
- Regular medications with dosage and directions
- Any allergies or medical conditions
- Your contact information (work and cell numbers)
- House address and phone number
- Pediatrician name and contact information
- Preferred hospital and pharmacy with phone numbers
- Another emergency adult contact
- Poison control (1-800-222-1222)

Ingestions

83. My child ate berries off a plant, swallowed a pill I accidentally dropped, drank dishwasher soap, (fill in the blank). What do I do?

Repeat after me…**1-800-222-1222.** Always keep the number for poison control handy (on your fridge, near a house phone, and in your cell phone) for such emergencies. If you have any information about what your child ingested (such as color, shape, or markings on a pill), let them know. If not, give them as much information as you can. They will instruct you on what to do. It is no longer recommended to give syrup of ipecac to make your child throw up—sometimes that can cause further harm.

Of course, if your child is not acting well or it is a true emergency, call 911. If you have any other questions or concerns, call your pediatrician.

84. What should I do—I think my child swallowed a coin!

As long as your child is acting normally (ie, can breathe and talk and drink fine), try not to panic. Most coins smaller than a quarter will pass right through without getting stuck. Touch base with your pediatrician, who may advise you to check your child's stool for a few days until you find the coin. If it doesn't come out the other end, a doctor may have to go looking for it. A simple x-ray film can tell exactly where the coin is and whether a specialist needs to retrieve it. If your child is in diapers, it's easy to search for loose change. If he is toilet trained, have him go on a paper plate, or loosely plastic-wrap the toilet to catch the poop. Isn't parenting fun?

If your child is choking, having trouble breathing, drooling, or in pain (in the mouth, throat, or tummy), call 911. For swallowed quarters or anything larger, batteries, magnets, or sharp objects such as a pin, call your doctor or head to the emergency department. If you aren't sure, call your pediatrician for advice.

> ## PEDIATRIC POINT
> ### Up the Nose or In the Ear
>
> Kids love to put beads, peas, you name it up their nose or in their ear. I can't tell you how many I've retrieved. Objects up the nose or in the mouth can be serious because if inhaled, they can interfere with breathing. It is less dangerous if an object is placed in the ear because the eardrum protects it from going too far. But wherever Sammy hid his veggies, they must be removed to avoid complications such as bleeding or infection. See your pediatrician as soon as possible.

Injuries

85. Help! My daughter fell off the couch. I think she hit her head. What should I do?

Newborn

Even though newborns rarely roll over on their own, they can wiggle and squirm, which is how they somehow manage to fall off couches and changing tables when parents turn away…even for just a moment. So after the loud thud is heard throughout the house, how do you know if she is truly injured? Usually a baby will cry immediately and then calm down when picked up and comforted by a parent. Once she is calm, use your hand and gently press all over her body for any tender areas that make her cry. If anything seems to hurt or if the initial crying persists, she should be evaluated right away.

Call 911 if your baby is unconscious or seriously injured. Otherwise, call your pediatrician and explain what happened. The doctor may want to see your child in the office or have you take her to the emergency department, especially for falls that occur from a height higher than a bed or couch or if your child is continuously crying, vomiting, or later is not feeding or acting as usual.

To prevent falls, buckle the safety strap on the changing table, don't leave a baby alone on a bed or couch, and never put a baby in a bouncy seat or car seat on an elevated surface such as a table or countertop.

Infant

Toddler

Luckily most falls, whether off beds or couches or while walking or running, do not result in serious injury. The most common cause for concern is head trauma and unless you saw her fall, it may not be apparent if your child hit her head. If your child loses consciousness after the fall, she needs to be evaluated as soon as possible, so see your pediatrician or go to the emergency department. If she cries for a moment and then continues playing, your pediatrician may ask you to closely observe her at home. Check her scalp. Large goose-egg bumps are typically a sign of injury on the outside of the skull, not inside where the brain is. If she'll let you, apply ice (or a bag of frozen peas or corn) wrapped in a cloth for a few minutes to help soothe the pain and

decrease the swelling. As long as she is acting all
right, your doctor will probably say that there's
no need to wake her up throughout the night
to check on her.

 Call your pediatrician or go to the emergency
department if your child begins complaining of a
severe headache, crying uncontrollably, vomiting,
or talking, walking, or acting abnormally. Also, if
there is a cut that won't stop bleeding with 5 minutes of direct pressure, call your pediatrician.

86. My toddler was running, tripped, and fell. Now he is crying and won't walk. How do I know if he broke something?

You can't know for sure. Even doctors can't always tell without an x-ray film. If it happens during office hours, you
can always call for an appointment. More often than not,
such injuries seem to happen after hours or on the weekend. Before you rush to the emergency department, give
the situation a few minutes and try to comfort him. Once
he calms down, give him an appropriate dose of ibuprofen
(Motrin or Advil) or acetaminophen (Tylenol) and ice the
injury if he'll let you. If there is an obvious deformity
where the injury occurred or he continues to scream in
pain and refuses to stand or walk, it's best to have him evaluated (you're probably warming up your car as you read this
anyway). If your child seems fine or it's late at night, it's OK
to wait until the next morning for the injury to be evaluated.
He may get better and start walking again on his own.

When the next day comes, if your child is walking around normally, don't worry about it. Your toddler probably just had a minor injury (not a fracture or break) that has already healed. If he's still limping or seems to be in pain, make an appointment with your pediatrician. The doctor may order an x-ray film to look for a toddler fracture (tiny break in the lower leg bone that commonly occurs in toddlers). It isn't a serious condition but does need to be immobilized, usually with a cast for a few weeks to heal properly.

87. I picked up my child by her arms and now she's holding one by her side, won't move it, and cries when I try to touch it. Did I break something?

This common injury is called a nursemaid elbow. Any sudden upward pull on a child's arm can cause the elbow to come out of the joint, which is called a dislocation. Luckily, your pediatrician should be able to put the arm back into place in the office with a simple arm maneuver. (After I fix such an injury, I like to place a lollipop in the hand of the previously injured arm and leave the room. I check back in 5 minutes and the child is always happily licking the lollipop, which means the arm is now fine.) Although there are no long-term complications from this injury, because the ligaments are temporarily slightly stretched, some toddlers may be prone to the elbow dislocating again. So Mommy and Daddy need to take a break from playing helicopter. In the future, pick your child up under the arms or around the chest to avoid this problem.

Car Seats

Automobile crashes are the number one cause of death in children. While you can't control others on the road, you can make sure that your family always buckles up safely. Don't forget to have your car seat checked by a trained professional. Proper use and installation is key to protecting your little one during an accident.

88. I'm so confused. Which car seat is best for my child?

You're not alone. With so many choices available, there isn't one seat that is the "best" or "safest," so car seat confusion is common. The best seat is simply the one that fits your child's size, is correctly installed, and is used properly every time you drive. Don't forget to have your car seat installation checked by a trained professional (many police or fire stations will inspect car seats).

Newborn

If you haven't already bought your infant car seat, you will need one to safely transport your newborn home from the hospital. Many parents like to start with an infant-only car seat because the base can be left in the car (you can buy extra bases if you have more than one car) and the seat clicks in and out of the base for easy transport of your little one. The car seat must be rear-facing in the backseat at all times. If this is your first child (and the only car seat in your car), the rear center seat is recommended if possible (some cars may not be equipped for a car seat in the center). If you need to put 2 car seats in back, the most comfortable fit may be to have one on each side.

Infant

As your infant grows, he will outgrow the infant-only car seat, which leaves many parents wondering what to buy next. Check the weight and height limit on your infant seat to know when he will need a new car seat. A convertible car seat is usually the next step. As the name implies, it can be used rear-facing now, then when he is older, it can be turned around to become a forward-facing car seat.

Toddler

According to many state laws, when your child reaches both 1 year of age and 20 pounds, you can turn his car seat around so it is forward-facing in the backseat of your car. According to safety experts and the American Academy of Pediatrics, children younger than 2 years should remain rear-facing until they reach the maximum weight or height allowed by the car seat. There's no question that rear-facing is definitely the safest way for a child younger than 2 to ride.

Cuts, Scrapes, and Bites...Oh My!

89. How do I know if my child needs stitches?

Cuts and scrapes are common injuries for active kiddos. A cut that is deep, has gaping skin, or won't stop bleeding after 10 minutes of constant, direct pressure may need stitches to close the wound. On some areas of the body, glue (like super glue, but safe for skin) or staples (again, specially made for skin, usually the scalp) can be used instead. Take your child's immunization records with you; she may need a tetanus shot depending on what caused the injury and when she had her last tetanus booster.

If you think your child has a cut that needs to be medically closed, call your pediatrician to find out if this can be done in the office or if you need to see an emergency department doctor or a plastic surgeon. Don't wait too long—it's often best to take care of a cut within 4 to 8 hours of the injury. Signs of infection such as fever, redness, pain, swelling, or pus also need to be evaluated ASAP.

FUN FACT
Getting Out Splinters

Clean the area well with soap and water. You can then try to remove the splinter with tweezers by grabbing the protruding end and pulling gently. If you can't get it out, wait a few days to see if it works itself out.

 If the splinter is deep or doesn't come out soon on its own, or there are signs of infection such as redness, swelling, oozing, or pain, please be sure to see your pediatrician.

90. An insect bit/stung my son and now his leg is swollen and red. What should I do?

Ouch! First look and see if there is any visible stinger. If so, remove it by gently scraping horizontally across the skin with the edge of a credit card or clean fingernail. Wash the area with soap and water and apply ice or a cool compress to help decrease the pain and swelling. You can also give an appropriate dose of ibuprofen (if the child is older than 6 months) or acetaminophen for pain. If it seems itchy, you can try a topical anti-itch medication (like hydrocortisone cream or calamine lotion) or give an appropriate dose of an antihistamine. Ask your pediatrician if you are unsure what the proper dose is for your child.

 If there are any signs of a secondary skin infection such as increasing redness, pain, drainage, or pus, see your pediatrician because treatment with an antibiotic may be needed. In addition, if there are any signs of a serious allergic reaction to the bite or sting such as trouble breathing or swallowing or giant hives (welts), seek medical attention immediately!

CHAPTER 11

Growing Up

"Walking and talking"

Every new thing your child does, from her first smile to her first step, is exciting and monumental. You may quickly realize, though, that your little one's timing may not be exactly the same as others of the same age. As a parent it is only natural to compare your child to others. No matter how many times you are told to resist the urge to compare, you just can't. I won't pretend I can convince you to stop, but I will attempt to ease your mind by reassuring you that each and every child is unique and different in her own way. You will always meet a parent whose child got her first tooth, took her first steps, said her first word, used the potty on her own, and sat quietly in circle time and listened before yours was even close to becoming ready.

Keeping that in mind, I hope you will appreciate every moment and milestone your own infant or toddler reaches and continue to play an active role in her development. I'm not going to sugarcoat it—there will be good days and bad days. But each day is a new day, full of new opportunities for learning and growing.

Growth

91. When should I expect to see teeth and how do I care for them?

Infant

The first tooth usually appears around 6 to 8 months of age, although some children won't get their first tooth until after 1 year of age. Once that first tooth appears, gently wipe it off with a soft washcloth or toothbrush before bed. After 6 months of age, a little fluoride is needed to help prevent cavities. Depending on the concentration of fluoride in your water supply, your pediatrician may recommend a fluoride vitamin or simply giving your infant some water with fluoride every day.

Toddler

Around 1 year, gently brush your child's teeth with water or a tiny bit of non-fluoride toothpaste. Make brushing his teeth a fun game. Get 3 toothbrushes so your toddler can hold one in each hand while you brush with the third. Anytime around age 1 year is a good time to see a pediatric dentist. The dentist will let you know if your child needs extra fluoride via water, vitamin, or toothpaste. Follow the exact recommendation because too much fluoride can cause permanent white spots on the teeth. Around age 2, start letting your toddler brush as well, although you will be doing most of the work. Play a game and take turns. Count to 10 while he attempts to brush, then count to 10 while you brush, and go back and forth a few times. Another idea is to sing a favorite song. A pea-sized amount of fluoride toothpaste can be used after your toddler can master rinsing and spitting, typically after age 2 or 3.

 If your child's first tooth doesn't appear by 1 year of age or if his teeth look discolored or otherwise not normal, call your pediatrician for a referral to a pediatric dentist.

92. When does my baby need shoes? Will special shoes help her feet so they don't turn in or out?

Shoes protect your child's feet when she walks on unsafe surfaces or if they need to be covered due to weather conditions (rain, sun, or snow). I know those designer shoes you bought are cute, but it's really best to leave your baby barefoot; infants learn to walk by gripping the ground with their feet in a heel-to-toe pattern (much easier to do when barefoot). Shoes will not help your child learn to walk sooner, better, or faster. Once you do look for shoes, make sure the shoe is comfortable and flexible and has traction and room for growth. It's best to have a trained professional help find the right fit for your infant or toddler.

In general, as infants begin to walk, their feet turn slightly outward; over time they may even turn slightly inward; and with more time they eventually straighten out. Special shoes or braces are typically no longer used for treatment. If you are concerned, let your pediatrician watch your child walk at your next visit.

Development

93. Should I be worried that my 4-month-old isn't rolling yet, my 6-month-old isn't sitting alone yet, or my 1-year-old isn't walking yet?

Every child grows and develops at different rates, which is why there is a wide age range for each milestone. In general, if it's only one milestone that your infant hasn't hit yet, he may just need a bit more time and encouragement. Pages 141 through 143 have a chart to help you know *approximately* what to expect as your child grows.

 Your pediatrician will evaluate your child's development at each well-child visit, but if you have any specific concerns or worries, call or schedule an appointment ASAP.

Developmental Milestones

Age	Gross Motor	Fine Motor	Language	Social
Newborns	• Head lags behind when pulled to sit. • Turns head to side. • After 1 month, able to follow objects to midline.	• Keeps hands tightly closed. • Holds objects placed in the palm.	• Cries.	• Regards faces.
2 months	• Lifts head 45 degrees when on tummy. • Follows objects past the midline with the eyes.	• No longer clenches fist tightly.	• Coos.	• Smiles at anything or anyone. • Recognizes parents.
3 months	• Able to hold head up. • Head still bobs when sitting.	• Swipes at objects. • Hands are held open at rest.	• Coos.	• Anticipates feeding.
4 months	• Pushes up chest with arms and lifts head when on tummy. • No head lag when pulled to a seated position. • Starts to roll from front to back.	• Brings hands to midline. • Grasps objects and brings them to mouth.	• Laughs.	• Responds to voice. • Enjoys looking at surroundings.

Developmental Milestones *(continued)*

Age	Gross Motor	Fine Motor	Language	Social
6 months	• Starts to sit without support. • May roll from back to front.	• Reaches with one or both hands. • Passes objects from one hand to the other. • Rakes small objects. • Grabs feet and pulls to mouth.	• Babbles.	• Excited to see and play with parents. • Begins to recognize person as unfamiliar.
9 months	• Gets into sitting position without help. • May crawl. • May pull to a stand. • May begin to walk while holding onto furniture (cruise).	• Holds bottle. • Uses thumb and a finger to grasp things (pincer grasp).	• Says "mama" and "dada" nonspecifically.	• Waves bye. • Claps. • Understands "no."
12 months	• Starts to stand without help. • Takes a few steps with help. • Begins to walk alone.	• Lets go of objects deliberately. • Attempts to scribble.	• Uses a few words other than mama or dada.	• Imitates. • Responds when called.

Developmental Milestones (continued)

Age	Gross Motor	Fine Motor	Language	Social
15 months	• Crawls up stairs. • Starts to walk backwards.	• Imitates scribbles. • Uses spoon and cup without help.	• Says 4 to 6 words.	• Follows one-step commands.
18 months	• Starts to run. • Able to throw ball without falling over.	• Scribbles spontaneously. • Turns pages, but several at a time.	• Says 8 to 20 words.	• Points to body parts. • Imitates tasks.
2 years	• Climbs up and down steps without help. • Kicks ball.	• Imitates lines when drawing. • Able to turn pages one at a time.	• Says 50 to 100 words. • Uses pronouns but incorrectly at first. • Says 2-word sentences.	• Follows 2-step commands. • Plays alongside another child but not together.
3 years	• Alternates feet when walking up stairs. • Rides/pedals tricycle.	• Copies a circle. • Undresses alone. • Tries to dress self.	• Combines 3 or more words into sentences. • Asks questions.	• Group play. • Begins to share and takes turns. • Knows name, age, gender.

94. What are the signs of autism?

Autism is a complex developmental disorder with a spectrum of symptoms that range from mild to severe. It is more common in boys and although signs can be found as early as infancy, it is typically noticed between 18 months and 3 years of age. Your pediatrician should screen for autism at the 18- and 24-month checkups, as well as survey your child's development at every well-child visit. It is also important to note that there are other developmental issues that may cause symptoms similar to autism. As always, talk to your pediatrician if you have any concerns about your child's development.

Here are some common signs of autism.

- Delayed or absent speech
- Lack of eye contact and response to name
- Lack of gestures such as pointing
- Doesn't like hugs and kisses
- Repetitive behavior or words
- Difficult behavior
- Delayed milestones, especially language and social skills
- Unusual reactions to the way things look, feel, smell, taste, or sound

 If you think your child may have an autism spectrum disorder, talk to your pediatrician. Early intensive therapy (eg, speech therapy, occupational therapy, behavioral therapy, social integration) can improve symptoms and bring about a substantial improvement.

PEDIATRIC POINT
Turn Off the Television!

The American Academy of Pediatrics recommends that children younger than 2 years not be exposed to television, videos, or video or computer games. The first 2 years of life are especially important in the growth and development of your child's brain. During this time, children need good, positive interaction with other children and adults. Too much television can negatively affect early brain development.

After age 2, limit your child to no more than 1 or 2 hours a day of educational, nonviolent screen time. Make sure programs are age appropriate and always watch or play games with your child so that you know the content and can discuss it. This is a perfect opportunity to teach your child life lessons and bring up important topics such as health and safety.

Behavior

95. What is the best way to deal with temper tantrums?

The key to discipline is consistency. Remember, you are the parent. Temper tantrums can be challenging to deal with, but they can also be minimized. Here are some tips you can use to help stop (or at least decrease) the tantrums.

- Ignore the behavior. If you walk away or don't pay attention, your child will likely stop.
- Time-out. Pick a location in your house where your child must sit or stand for a few minutes (1 minute per year of age) or until she calms down.

DR. TANYA'S TIP
Changing Behavior—It Takes a Week

Almost any behavior can be modified within 1 week as long as all caregivers are consistent and provide encouragement and praise. Whether you're trying to stop your toddler from biting or getting him to sleep all night in a big-boy bed, 1 week is usually all you need—as long as you stick with it.

- **Be** consistent—have all caregivers keep the same rules and routine.
- **En**courage—read an encouraging book on the topic or tell a story.
- **Ha**ve rewards—praise him for doing well; offer hugs and kisses, stickers, or a small token.
- **A**nticipate conflict—change your routine to avoid battle situations.
- **V**ery quick response—immediately follow your child's action with a consequence (good or bad).
- **I**gnore—minor, undesirable actions often aren't worth your energy.
- **O**ne at a time—pick your battle and choose only one behavior to modify at a time.
- **R**ole model—your child watches you and follows your lead so demonstrate good behavior, respect, and love to those around you.

- Refocus your child on something else. I like to walk to the other side of the room, announce "Mommy is going to read a book," and start reading out loud. My son usually quiets down and comes to join me.
- Provide praise when your child is behaving nicely. Catch her doing something good and reward her.

- Avoid situations that are likely to bring on a tantrum.
  If she always melts down on your second errand, limit
  each outing to one.
- Leave the location. If you are in a public place (eg, grocery
  store, restaurant) simply take her and leave. It's hard to do
  when you're in the checkout line or the middle of a meal,
  but it does work.

FUN FACT
Thumb Sucking

Thumb sucking is a very common self-soothing behavior
that usually begins in the first year of life. It isn't dangerous
and toddlers eventually outgrow it, usually by the time
they start kindergarten. You can't take the thumb away, but
you can try introducing another lovey or comfort item such
as a special toy or blanky. Applying adhesive strips, splints,
or yucky-tasting solutions isn't very effective at this age.
The best method of action is to ignore the behavior, take
comfort in the fact that your toddler has a quiet method
to soothe herself, and wait it out.

Potty Training

96. When can I toilet train my child and how do I do it?

Many children are ready to start when they are around 2½
years old, so ask your pediatrician when to start at your
child's 2-year checkup. Once you get the go-ahead, the first
thing to do is to take a deep breath and relax. Everyone
eventually learns how to use the potty. If your child isn't
ready or if you're feeling pressured by a preschool start date
or birth of a sibling, inevitably it won't happen and may

even take longer. If you wait until your toddler is truly ready, it's much easier on everyone involved. In case you are wondering, the age at which your toddler eventually learns how to use the toilet has no bearing on how smart he is or his future academic success. No college application or job interview is going to ask him at what age he learned. Signs that your toddler may be ready include the following:

- Stays dry for several hours at a time.
- Has regular, predictable bowel movements.
- Shows signs he is about to go in his diaper such as hiding or squatting.
- Seems uncomfortable when dirty and asks to be changed.
- Follows simple instructions, walks to the bathroom, and helps undress himself.
- Asks to use the toilet and wear big-kid underwear.

To be truly toilet trained, your toddler has to be able to sense that he needs to go, be able to interpret that sensation, and then be able to tell you and take some action (actually get the pee or poop in the potty). Typically, this happens around 2½ years but can be earlier or later.

Prepping for toilet training can actually begin earlier. Here are some steps to success.

Potty talk: Teach your child the words that your family will use for things like toilet, stool, and urine. (Potty, poop, and pee seem to be very acceptable these days, but be careful. Whatever words you use your child will repeat in public, possibly while grocery shopping.) Tell him what he just did or the action you are taking such as, "Jacob just went poop," or "Let's change your dirty diaper." Kids are smart. He will catch on quickly and start telling you when he goes or that he needs to be changed.

Soft stool: Make sure your child's stools are soft. If he is constipated and his stool is hard, he won't want to go in the potty because it hurts. He'll hold onto his stool, making it larger, harder, and more painful, and potty training will not be successful. (For stool-softening tips, see question #40, pages 59–60).

See one, do one: Make a point of announcing when you need to go and let him watch you use the bathroom. Teach him to always wash his hands after.

Big or little potty: It's up to you if you want to buy a smaller potty chair or just have a stool or toilet seat insert for him. Either way, it helps if he has something to push his feet against. Have you ever tried to poop with your feet off the ground? It's not easy.

Fun and games: Make the time fun for him—read a story or sing a song. There are several good books about using the potty that will encourage him. Try not to scold him for not going or force him to sit there. It works much better if you praise his efforts, however small they are. Reward with positive words, big hugs, kisses, or a special potty song or dance. If needed, you can always go the sticker, stamp, or small treat route as well.

> ## FUN FACT
> ### Dry at Night
>
> Potty training refers to daytime use of the toilet. Nighttime dryness for most kids doesn't happen until much later. In fact, it's perfectly normal for kids to still wet at night up until 6 years of age, and sometimes even longer. So use a pull-up or diaper at night (you can call it nighttime underwear) until your child is dry most nights.

97. My 3-year-old knows how, but will only use the toilet sometimes. I'm tired of alternating between underwear and pull-ups. What should I do?

If your child has had some success and knows what to do, then this may be a behavioral issue. It can be confusing for her to sometimes have big-girl underwear and other times diapers or pull-ups. Choose a long weekend where you can be home with her the entire time, let her know that starting tomorrow she gets to wear big-girl underwear all of the time, get rid of the diapers and pull-ups, buy a big stack of underwear, and go for it! Use a reward system such as a stamp on her hand or a phone call to grandma or grandpa every time she goes in the potty. If she has an accident, acknowledge it ("Oops, you had an accident."), have her help clean up ("Let's dump the poop in the potty and rinse your clothes in the sink."), and move on ("Next time let Mommy know and I'll help you get to the potty in time."). If you are consistent and don't go backwards (no diapers for car rides or trips to the store), she will probably be potty trained in less than a week.

CHAPTER 12

Sleep
"All night long"

Sleep is by far the most popular of the parenting workshops in my practice and definitely one of the most important. Who doesn't want a few more Zs every night? The reality is the first few weeks at home with your newborn you probably won't get much; the first few months can be hit or miss; but after that, if you play your cards right, you and your baby can start sleeping well—at least most of the time. So how do you stack the odds in your favor? Bedtime routine, consistency, and a little will power can make all the difference. That said, even the best-laid plans at 6:00 pm won't always go according to schedule at 4:00 am when you're sleep deprived and making quick decisions. But stay on track and keep your goal in mind—to sleep all night long.

While I have found success with the following techniques, your pediatrician can help make adjustments as needed for your child.

Sleep Solutions

98. I'm so exhausted. When will my baby sleep through the night and how can I make that happen?

I hear you. As I type this, my 2-month-old is napping beside me and neither of us slept much last night. My only solace is that I know his sleep schedule will improve and at around 4 to 6 months of age, he will hopefully be sleeping 8 hours a night. Here's the plan.

First 2 months of life: During this time, your baby still needs to feed when he wakes up every 3 to 4 hours. Start a regular bedtime routine so he can learn that this is night-time and not nap time. It doesn't need to be long. Something like bath (if it's bath night), pajamas, book, feed, swaddle, in bed, and lights out may work well. He'll probably fall asleep during the feed, or you'll rock him to sleep, which is fine for now.

Three to 4 months: Continue the bedtime routine, but end with placing your baby in his crib awake so he can learn how to put himself to sleep. If feeding always puts him to sleep, reverse your routine so you end with pajamas or story time. If he gets used to being rocked or fed to sleep, he will need you to perform these rituals when he wakes up in the middle of the night. When he does wake up in the middle of the night, give him a few minutes before you jump in and feed him. Often it's just a wakeful part of his sleep cycle and he'll drift off again on his own.

Four to 6 months: Your baby most likely does not need to feed anymore in the middle of the night, so he should be able to sleep for 6 to 8 hours (if you let him). Keep your bedtime routine consistent and allow him to fall asleep on his own. When he wakes up in the middle of the night, allow him to use the same self-soothing skills to put himself back to sleep. As you wean your baby from the night-time feed, he may cry a bit (or a lot) as he learns how to put himself back to sleep. Give him time to do this. Within a few nights he will figure out how to soothe himself back to sleep. Good sleep habits are important (for everyone in the house).

After 6 months: Your baby should be able to sleep at least 8 hours straight at night. If not, this is a good time to improve your bedtime routine and nighttime sleep plan (see question #99, pages 154–155).

PEDIATRIC POINT
Sudden Infant Death Syndrome

Sudden infant death syndrome (SIDS) is the unexplained death of an infant younger than 1 year. The exact cause is unknown. To decrease your baby's risk for SIDS, always put your baby to sleep on his back, don't expose your baby to cigarette smoke, and use a firm mattress without pillows, toys, or extra-soft bedding. While loose blankets are not recommended, sleep sacks and wearable blankets are good options to keep your baby warm while sleeping. Don't forget to remind grandparents and other caregivers of these recommendations.

99. My infant/toddler wakes up in the middle of the night and screams until I nurse her, rock her, bring her in my bed, or give her the pacifier. I can't bear to hear her cry. How can I get her to sleep through the night?

After 4 to 6 months of age, if you always nurse, rock, cuddle, or "pacifier" your baby in the middle of the night, she will always need your help to fall back to sleep. Nighttime is sleep time and unless you want to continue doing this for the next year or longer, give her the chance to learn how to put herself back to sleep. It's much easier now than when she's standing up in her crib yelling for mommy. Yes, she may scream and cry. I know it's hard for you to hear. I know you may be worrying, but you have all day to cuddle with her, show her how much you love her, and let her know that you're there for her. And since you're probably also wondering if she's hungry, she's not. It's just a habit. From 4 to 6 months of age she should easily be able to go 6 to 8 hours at night without food, and after 6 months of age most babies can go at least 8 to 10 hours. Once you stop feeding your child in the middle of the night, she'll make up for it by eating more during the day.

After 6 to 8 months of age, introduce a lovey (small blanky or stuffed animal) into her crib that she can cuddle with. Pick a night. Friday night often works well because the first few nights might be tough. Be consistent because she won't understand why sometimes she gets picked up and fed and sometimes she doesn't. Let her fall asleep at bedtime and tell her how long you expect her to sleep (saying it out loud helps you know your plan). When she does wake up, allow her to figure out how to get back to sleep on her own. There may be a few nights of crying, but if you resist the temptation to intervene, each night the crying will be less, and before you know it she'll be sleeping all night long (and so will you). In the morning, tell her how proud you are of her—clap, cheer, sing, or dance. Even if she is too young to understand, it's a good routine to start. Both parents must be on the same page for any sleep plan to work, so talk to your partner and agree on a consistent approach.

Toddler Troubles

100. My toddler wakes up at night, gets out of his bed, and comes into our room. If I try to put him back, he throws a fit and wakes up his siblings or the neighbors. What can I do?

For those of you reading this before your child moves into a big-kid bed, it's much easier and safer to sleep-train a toddler in a crib—before he can get out and roam around the house. No matter what the age, it's hard to let a child cry when you know that it will disturb others. Warn everyone in ear's reach (buy the neighbors a present) and spend a few consistent nights squelching the problem. Once your child is sleeping through the night, everyone will benefit.

Again, set aside a few nights in a row where it's OK if you don't get any sleep (maybe a long weekend). Keep your bedtime routine consistent. Let your child know what's expected of him—to sleep all night long in his own bed. Get him a special new pillow, blanky, or stuffed animal that he can cuddle with in the middle of the night. Let him know that it is there to help him sleep all night in his own big-boy bed. When he does get out, take his hand and march him back to bed. Simply say, "At night we sleep in our own bed." Tuck him in and leave. The next time he gets out, say "Bed."

Take his hand and march him back to bed. The third time, don't say anything. Just take him back to bed. Continue this routine every time he gets out of bed. The next night do the same thing. It should only take 3 or 4 nights in a row (allow an entire week…just in case) before you are all sleeping all night long in your own beds. You may want to put a safety gate at your child's door so you can leave the door open for you to hear him, but the gate will keep him from getting out and roaming around the house at night alone. In the morning, tell him how proud you are of him—dance, cheer, throw a party, whatever it takes to encourage everyone in the house to continue the routine.

DR. TANYA'S TIP
From Crib to Big-Kid Bed

- **B**uild excitement—find a book (or make up a story) on the topic to get your toddler ready. Include her in choosing bedding for her new big bed.
- **I**ncorporate "lovey"—explain that her special blanky, stuffed animal, or doll from her crib will sleep in her big bed too.
- **G**o for it—pick a night to have her start sleeping in the bed and don't go back.
- **B**edtime routine—keep your previous bedtime routine and be consistent.
- **E**ncourage good sleep habits—praise and reward her (hugs and kisses work well) at bedtime and every morning.
- **D**on't forget safety—install a bed rail or remove the bed from the frame so the mattress is low to ground. Keep her room safe in case she gets out of bed. Consider using a door gate for her bedroom to keep her from wandering the house.

101. My toddler wakes up at night and screams. Is she having nightmares? Or are these the night terrors I've heard about?

While both can be scary for parents and interrupt everyone's sleep, night terrors and nightmares are very different.

Night terrors usually occur in children older than 18 months, usually in the first third of the night. The typical scenario is a child who wakes up approximately 3 hours after going to sleep, acting like she is possessed. She may scream, shake, and point at things. She is not comforted by parents and doesn't even know they are in the room, but goes easily back to sleep after the episode. The next morning the child doesn't remember the event, although everyone else in the house will. Stress and tiredness can contribute to night terrors. What can you do to break the cycle? Because night terrors generally occur around the same time every night, wake your child up about 15 to 30 minutes prior to the expected episode. This will break her sleep cycle and her body will jump into the next stage of sleep when the terrors don't occur. Also, make sure your child is not overtired. Put her to bed a little earlier at night or make sure she gets a nap if she still needs one.

Nightmares typically happen during the second half of the night. Kids with nightmares will wake up fully and respond to parental comforting. They may remember the dream, even the next day. Reassurance each time your child has a nightmare can help prevent them from happening again. Talk to your child about the dreams and explain that they are not real. Take a look at your child's environment (eg, preschool, home) and see if there is anything bothering her.

Be sure to avoid exposing your child to violent activity, movies, or television shows. Talk to your pediatrician if the nightmares persist for more than a few days.

Index

Ettus, Samantha, iii
The Experts' Guide to the Baby Years (Ettus), iii
Eye infections, 91–92

F

Falls, 128–130
Febrile seizures, 84–85
Feeding issues, 39–54. *See also specific*
Fenugreek capsules, milk supply and, 24
Fever, 73–85, 115. *See also* Temperature
   behavior and, 77
   calling pediatrician on, 63, 74, 77, 78, 80, 88
   causes of, 74–75
     teething as, 82
   following immunizations, 83–84
   managing, 79–80
     popsicles in, 82
   viral, 78
Fine motor skills, developmental milestones in, 141–143
First aid, 125–135
Flat heads, preventing, 13
Flu, stomach, 60, 65
Fluids, recipe for keeping down, 71
Fluoride
   dental care and, 138
   in water supply, 34
Flu vaccine, 100
Fontanelle, sunken, 72
Food allergies, 47
   introducing solid foods and, 45–46
   symptoms of, 47
Food Fights: Winning the Nutritional Challenges of Parenthood Armed With Insight, Humor, and a Bottle of Ketchup (Jana and Shu), 49
Foods
   as cause of hives, 120–121
   solid, 44–47
   stage 2 baby, 46
   trials of new, 49

Insect bites/stings, 134–135
International Board Certified Lactation Consultant, 18
Iron in formula, 32–33
Irritability, 74

J

Jaundice, 19
    breastfeeding and, 109
    skin and, 108–110
*Just Tell Me What to Say: Sensible Tips and Scripts for Perplexed
        Parents* (Braun), iv

K

Karp, Harvey, 7

L

Lactation consultant, 1, 26
    certified, 18
    enlisting advice of, 25
Lactose-free milk, 62
La Leche League, 19
Language skills, developmental milestones in, 141–143
Lanolin cream, 25
Latch-on, improper, 26
Laxatives, natural, 59
Levalbuterol for coughing and wheezing, 97–98
Lice, head, 122
Liquid concentrate formula, 33
LiquiLyte, 70
    managing diarrhea with, 62

M

Medications. *See also* Antibiotics; *specific*
    accidental overdose of, 80
    antifungal, 112
    antiviral, 100
    for asthma, 97–98, 99
    avoiding mistakes with, 82

Tummy ache. *See* Stomachaches
2% milk, 52
Tylenol. *See* Acetaminophen (Tylenol)

U

Ulcers, mouth, 96
Ultrasound in diagnosing appendicitis, 69
Umbilical cord stump
    calling pediatrician if red, 11
    care of, 10–11
Umbilical granuloma, 10
Underwear, 150
Upper respiratory tract infections, 97
Urate crystals, 16
Urinary tract infections, risk of, and circumcision, 13
Urine stream, straight, 15

V

Vaccines, 103–105
    fever following, 83–84
    flu, 100
    against rotavirus, 61
    safety of, 104
    side effects from, 104
Vaporizer, congestion in infant and, 12
Vaseline, 110
Vegetables, introducing, 46
Viral fevers, 78
Viral infections, 78
Vitamin D–fortified milk, 50
Vitamin D supplementation, 21, 50
Vitamins
    infant, 21
    toddler, 50
Vomiting
    in newborn, 69–70
    projectile, 70
    in toddlers, 70–71